IC

PE

CA

ASIA

PACIFIC

OCEAN

INDIAN   OCEAN

AUSTRALASIA

OCEAN

TICA

Published 1982 by
The Hamlyn Publishing Group Limited
London · New York · Sydney · Toronto
Astronaut House, Feltham, Middlesex, England.
© Copyright The Hamlyn Publishing Group Limited 1982

ISBN 0 600 39500 6
Printed in Italy

My Favourite
PICTURE ATLAS

Roy Woodcock

Hamlyn
London · New York · Sydney · Toronto

Photographs

British Petroleum, London 24–25; J. Allan Cash, London 12; Bruce Coleman – Jen & Des Bartlett 67; Bruce Coleman – Douglas Botting 33; Bruce Coleman – Brian Coates 65 bottom inset; Bruce Coleman – Eric Crighton 23 left; Bruce Coleman – Gerald Cubitt 32 right; Bruce Coleman – Nicholas Devore 65 top inset; Bruce Coleman – Francisco Erize contents page; Bruce Coleman – Wedigo Ferchland 66; Bruce Coleman – Jennifer Fry 36 right; Bruce Coleman – Charles Henneghien 43 top; Bruce Coleman – Peter Jackson 35 right; Bruce Coleman – Norman Myers 37 right; Bruce Coleman – Dieter & Mary Plage 13, 40–41; Bruce Coleman – Jaroslav Poncar 43 centre left; Bruce Coleman – Norman Tomalin 51 bottom right; Colour Library International, London 10–11, 18 top left, 20–21, 23 right, 27 top, 28–29, 29, 32 left, 38 top, 38 bottom left, 38 bottom right, 39 bottom, 48 inset, 48, 50 bottom, 51 bottom left, 63 top, 63 inset, 68 bottom; Documentation Française, Paris 20; D. M. Halford, London 53 centre; Hamlyn Group Picture Library 22 top; Alan Hutchinson Library, London 51 top; Luiz Claudio Marigo, Rio de Janeiro 41 top right, 41 bottom, 54–55, 55 top, 58–59; Mittet Foto, Oslo 21 right; NASA, Washington, D.C. 9; Natural History Photographic Agency – Peter Johnson 47 left; G. R. Roberts, Todd's Valley 18 bottom left, 21 left, 24 top, 50 top, 62 top, 62 bottom, 64, 68 top; Royal Netherlands Embassy, London 22 bottom; Solarfilm, Reykjavik 14–15; South Australian Government 63 bottom; Judy Todd, London 24 centre, 27 bottom right, 55 bottom, 56–57, 64 centre left, 64 centre right, 64 bottom; Mireille Vautier, Paris 59 bottom left; Vautier-Decool, Paris 52, 59 top, 59 bottom right; Vautier – De Nanxe, Paris 53 top; ZEFA (UK), London 65; ZEFA (UK) – D. Baglin 61; ZEFA (UK) – S. Bardos 28 bottom; ZEFA (UK) – B. Benjamin 27 bottom left; ZEFA (UK) – K. Benser 36 left; ZEFA (UK) – David Corke 30; ZEFA (UK) – Bob Croxford 35 left; ZEFA (UK) – Damm title page; ZEFA (UK) – Kurt Goebel 55 centre, 56 inset; ZEFA (UK) – Hektor 30–31; ZEFA (UK) – Konrad Helbig 44; ZEFA (UK) – Hoffmann-Burchardi 34 bottom, 39 top; ZEFA (UK) – Karl Kummels 53 bottom; ZEFA (UK) – Leidmann 43 bottom; ZEFA (UK) – Colin Maher 18 right; ZEFA (UK) – Richard Nicholas 24 bottom; ZEFA (UK) – Neville Presho 34 top; ZEFA (UK) – Ingrid Rangnow 52–53; ZEFA (UK) – G. Ricatto 41 top left; ZEFA (UK) – Starfoto 43 centre right; ZEFA (UK) – H. Strass 57; ZEFA (UK) – Peter Thiele 37 left; ZEFA (UK) – B. Tosovic 31; ZEFA (UK) – Vontin 45; ZEFA (UK) – H. Woelk 28 top.

Cover photographs: Left Bruce Coleman – Nicholas Devore; Centre Judy Todd; Right Bruce Coleman – Gerald Cubitt.

Illustrations by
Linden Artists Ltd.
Tudor Art Agency Ltd.
Michael Youens

Maps by
Creative Cartography Ltd.

Contents

Our Place in Space

We live on a planet called Earth which is shaped like a ball. Five or six hundred years ago most people thought that the Earth was flat, like a plate, and that if you travelled too far in any direction you would fall off the edge. Now we know that we can journey right around the Earth and end up where we started.

Earth seems a very large place to us, but it is only one small planet in a group of planets called the Solar System. The nine planets in the Solar System all revolve around a central star which we call the Sun. (The difference between a star and a planet is that stars give off heat and light whereas planets do not.)

Our Sun is just one of many millions of stars in a huge system called a galaxy. The Sun is not even one of the biggest stars in our Galaxy. Compared to some stars it is quite

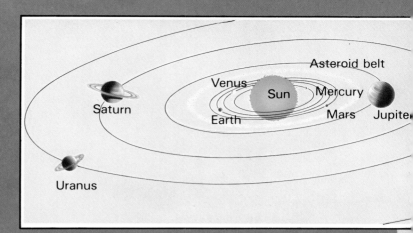

Above: *The planets of the Solar System, along with smaller pieces of debris, go round and round the Sun.*

small. Astronomers (people who study the stars) estimate that there are about 100 000 million stars in our Galaxy and that there may be as many as 10 000 million galaxies! We call all the galaxies, together with the empty space and the clouds of dust and gas between them, the Universe.

It is quite amazing to think what a tiny, insignificant place Earth is in comparison with the vastness of the Universe.

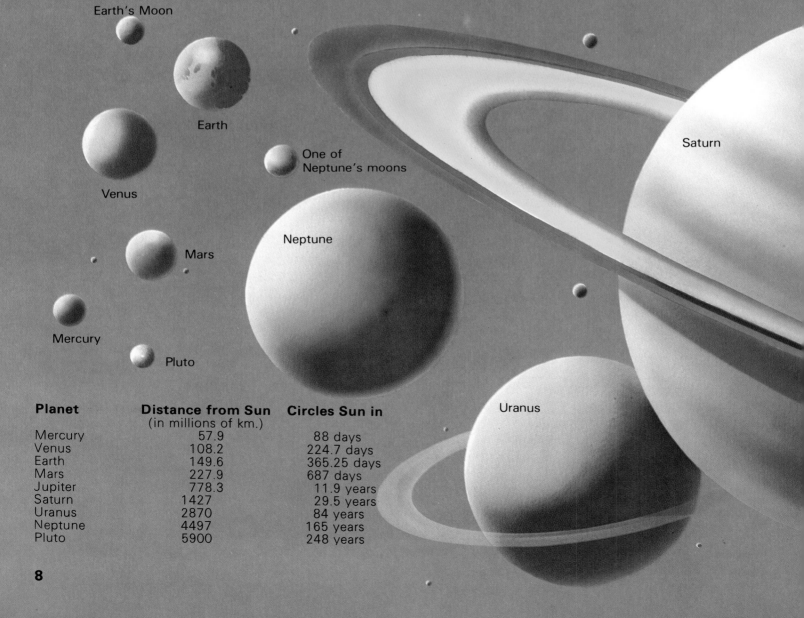

Planet	Distance from Sun (in millions of km.)	Circles Sun in
Mercury	57.9	88 days
Venus	108.2	224.7 days
Earth	149.6	365.25 days
Mars	227.9	687 days
Jupiter	778.3	11.9 years
Saturn	1427	29.5 years
Uranus	2870	84 years
Neptune	4497	165 years
Pluto	5900	248 years

Neptune

Pluto

Jupiter

Gravity

It is easy to see why people thought that the Earth was flat. They couldn't understand how anyone could live on the 'other side' of the Earth without falling off! Nothing can 'fall off' the Earth though because of a force called gravity.

Gravity works in the same way as a magnet pulls or 'attracts' pieces of iron towards it. The Earth's gravitational field pulls everything heavier than air down towards the Earth's surface. That is why, when you drop something, it falls to the ground and doesn't fly upwards.

Above: *The Earth's gravitational pull keeps our Moon from drifting off into space. It also holds in place the atmosphere which is a layer of gases around the Earth. The Sun has a gravitational pull of its own which keeps the planets of the Solar System in orbit around it. In space the gravitational pull is much less strong and an astronaut can 'float' outside his spaceship.*

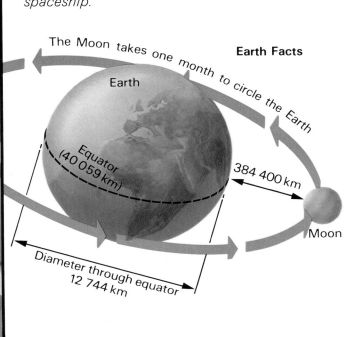

The Moon takes one month to circle the Earth

Earth Facts

Earth

Equator (40 059 km)

384 400 km

Moon

Diameter through equator 12 744 km

The Planet's of the Solar System showing their relative sizes.

The Earth in Motion

The Earth is never still. It moves through space at more than 100 000 kilometres an hour, circling round the Sun. It takes the Earth $365\frac{1}{4}$ days to complete one journey, or orbit, around the Sun. We use this period to measure time on Earth, calling 365 days, one year. Every fourth year the extra quarters are added together to make a year which has 366 days — a leap year.

As well as travelling around the Sun, the Earth also spins round and round, rather like a top. We say that the Earth rotates on its axis The Earth's axis is an imaginary line running through the centre of the Earth. The ends of the axis are the spots called the North Pole and South Pole.

We talk about the Sun rising and setting because it looks to us as if the Sun 'rises' in the morning, travels across the sky and 'sinks' in the evening. But it is really the Earth which is moving and not the Sun.

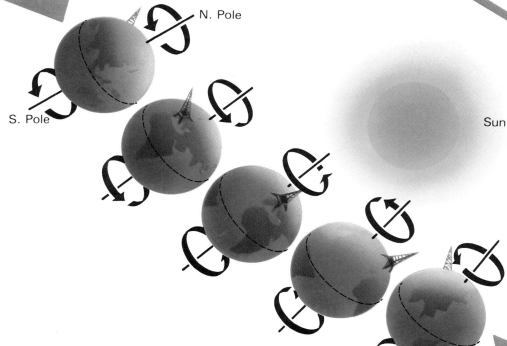

N. Pole

S. Pole

Earth's orbit

Sun

Day and Night
The Earth makes one complete turn every 24 hours. This means that at different times of the day, different parts of the Earth's surface are facing the Sun. When a country is facing the Sun, it is daytime in that part of the world. When that part of the Earth turns away from the Sun it is night and dark.

Earth's orbit

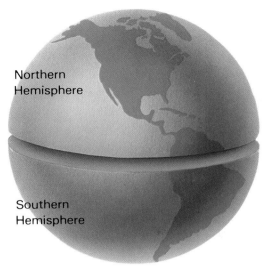

Northern
Hemisphere

Southern
Hemisphere

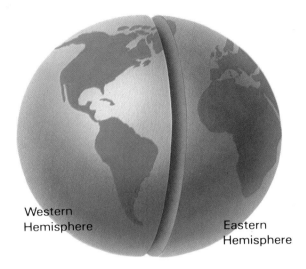

Western
Hemisphere

Eastern
Hemisphere

Dividing the Earth

The Earth is a sphere. A sphere is something round like a ball. The Earth can be divided into halves called hemispheres. Europe and North America are both in the Northern Hemisphere but Europe is in the Eastern Hemisphere and North America in the Western. The equator is an imaginary line around the middle of the Earth, dividing the Northern and Southern Hemispheres.

The Earth's Axis

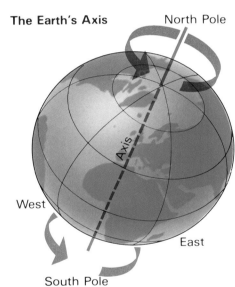

North Pole

Axis

West

East

South Pole

If you look carefully at this diagram of the Earth and its imaginary axis, you can see that the Earth is tilted slightly. This tilt means that, as the Earth travels around the Sun, different parts of the Earth are tilted closer to the Sun and therefore receive more heat and light. When a country is tilted towards the Sun it is summer in that region. When it is tilted away, it is winter.

The Seasons

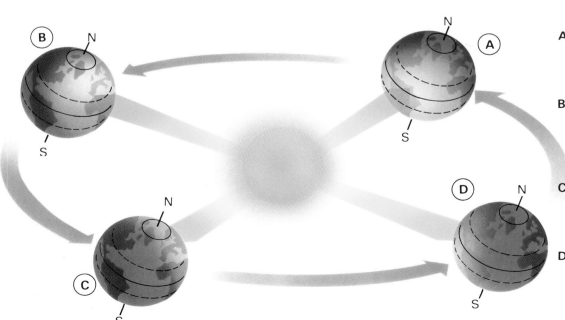

A March – it is spring in the Northern Hemisphere and autumn in the Southern Hemisphere

B June – the North Pole is tilted towards the Sun and it is summer in the Northern Hemisphere, winter in the Southern Hemisphere

C September – it is autumn in the Northern Hemisphere and Spring in the Southern Hemisphere

D December – the South Pole is tilted towards the Sun and it is summer in the Southern Hemisphere and winter in the Northern Hemisphere

Weather and Climate

The weather changes with the seasons in most parts of the world, with summers being warmer than winters. The only places without seasons are those near the equator where it is hot all the year round. This is because the rays of the Sun hit this region most directly.

The area around the equator is called the Tropical Region or Tropics. Because it is always hot here, air rises to form an area of low pressure. Low pressure means that the air

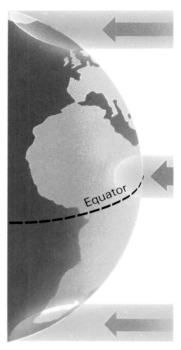

Above: *The Sun's rays lose heat passing through the atmosphere, so the more direct their journey, the greater the heat which reaches the Earth's surface. At the equator, where the rays strike vertically, they give most warmth.*

Left: *A rainstorm in Penang, Malaysia.*

Major Winds of the World

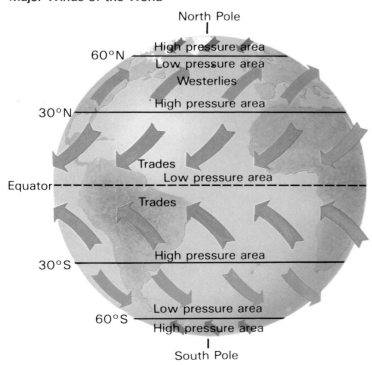

is rising and spreading out, so that the weight of the atmosphere is lighter than average. When this air rises, it cools and forms clouds and may give rain. The hottest places around the equator are also wet places where it rains nearly every day.

The air which rises near the equator falls down to Earth again just outside the Tropics. This falling air forms high pressure regions and the extra air spreads out across the Earth — as winds. In addition to the falling air of the Tropics there is also falling air in the Arctic and Antarctic because it is so cold.

The major winds of the world are all the result of air moving out from high pressure systems towards low pressure areas. But winds are also affected by the rotation of the Earth. All winds in the Northern Hemisphere are turned to their right by this rotation effect and in the Southern Hemisphere they are turned to their left.

The Earth's Crust

Our planet probably formed from a mass of whirling gases and dust over 4 500 million years ago. When this mass came together it formed a red-hot, molten ball. Gradually the outside of the ball cooled to form a crust, just like the crust on a baked pie, giving the Earth a solid surface.

Under this crust the Earth has many layers at many different temperatures and pressures. The very centre, or core, is solid because the

The Himalayan Mountains

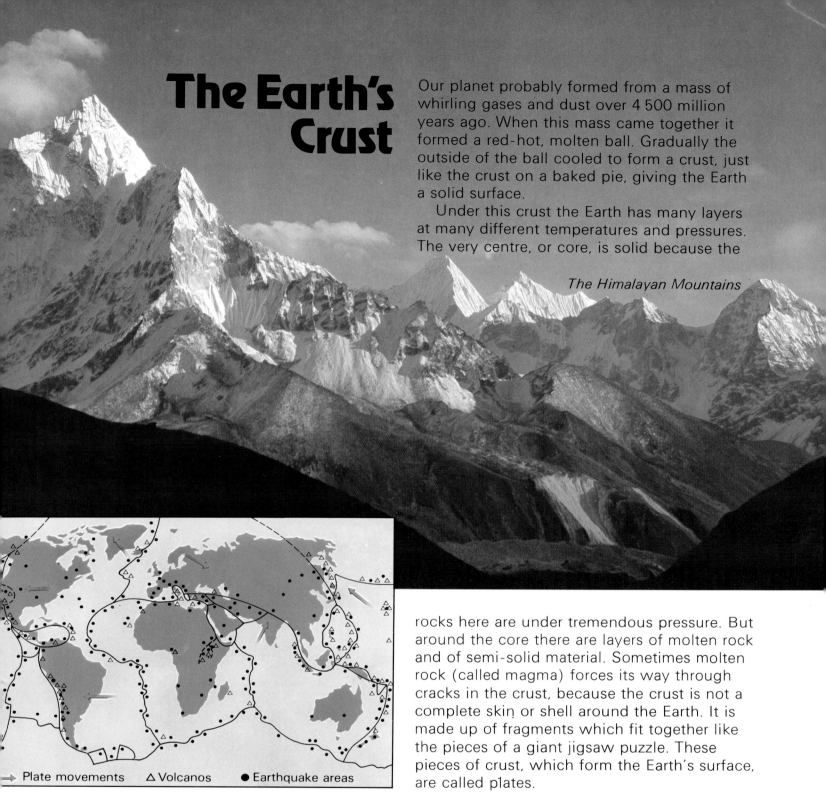

rocks here are under tremendous pressure. But around the core there are layers of molten rock and of semi-solid material. Sometimes molten rock (called magma) forces its way through cracks in the crust, because the crust is not a complete skin or shell around the Earth. It is made up of fragments which fit together like the pieces of a giant jigsaw puzzle. These pieces of crust, which form the Earth's surface, are called plates.

→ Plate movements   △ Volcanos   ● Earthquake areas

Above: *The Earth's crust is made up of pieces. Volcanos and earthquakes are common around the edges.*

Below: *When the plates move the movements cause different effects on the Earth's surface.*

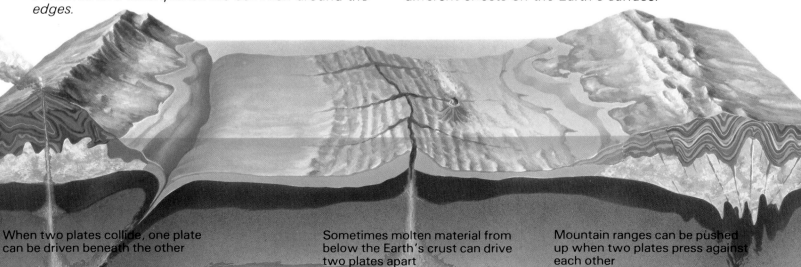

When two plates collide, one plate can be driven beneath the other

Sometimes molten material from below the Earth's crust can drive two plates apart

Mountain ranges can be pushed up when two plates press against each other

Continents on the Move

Studies of the crust which forms the ocean floors have shown that it moves and often carries land masses with it, like the passengers on a raft. The moving crust is the raft and the continents are the passengers.

A German geologist (someone who studies the rocks of which the Earth is formed and the changes they undergo) called Alfred Wegener wrote a book in 1915 in which he claimed that Africa and South America must have been joined together sometime in the past. You can imagine this quite easily if you look at the map at the front of this book and see how snugly they would fit together.

A great deal of research done since then, involving studies of the rock formations in South America and Africa, all goes to support Wegener's theory. Many geologists now believe that at one time all the land masses on Earth were joined and have gradually drifted apart.

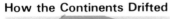

How the Continents Drifted

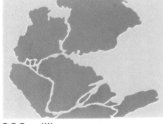

200 million years ago

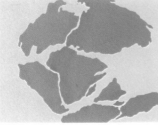

100 million years ago

50 million years ago

The world today – the continents are still moving very slowly

Lava flows

Layers of ash and lava

Central vent

Dyke

Magma

Section through a Volcano

What is a Map?

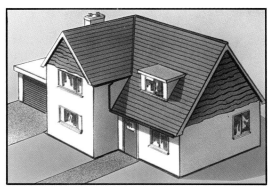

This is a picture of a house. The house is in a street, in a town, in the south of England.

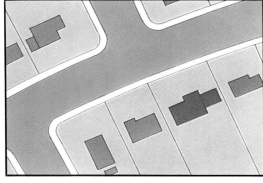

This is a map of the house and the street. A map gives an aerial view — as if you were floating up in the air and looking down.

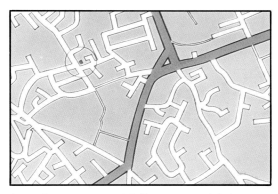

Imagine you could float even higher above the house. Now you could look down and draw a map of all the streets around the house.

From even higher up the house would be difficult to spot, but you could see all the roads, railways and countryside around it.

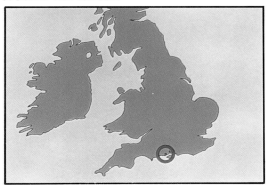

Higher still and you could map the whole of England and some of the neighbouring countries.

Higher again and the map includes the whole of Europe and the seas around the continent.

Above: *The island of Surtsey 'appeared' off Iceland in the 1960s, formed from material thrown up from below the Earth's crust. Surtsey is located where two plates appear to be moving apart, allowing molten rock to well up from below.*

Geyser

Right: *How much detail a map shows and how big an area it covers depends on its scale. These two maps show the same area but one is drawn to a larger scale than the other.*

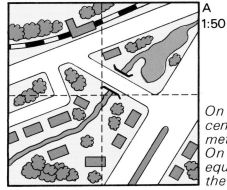

On map A one centimetre equals 50 metres on the ground. On map B one centimetre equals 200 metres on the ground.

Mapping a Round World

The world is shaped like a ball, but we usually see maps of the Earth's surface on a flat piece of paper. Try drawing a picture on an orange and then peeling off the skin. To get the picture to lie flat you have to split the skin leaving gaps in your picture.

The same thing happens when maps of the world are drawn. They cannot be drawn accurately on to a flat piece of paper without 'cheating' by stretching some parts of the map and shrinking others or by leaving big gaps.

Map projections are the methods map-makers use for adjusting maps from their shape on the globe to a flat piece of paper. All map projections distort the shape of the world in one way or another.

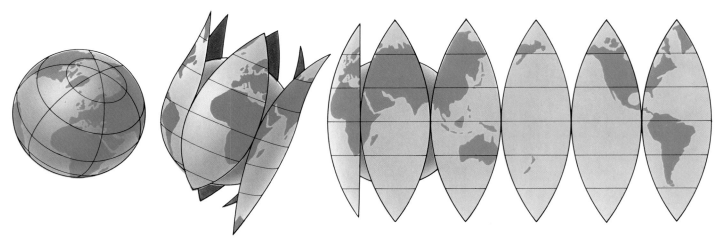

Latitude and Longitude

Map-makers and geographers use an imaginary pattern of lines on the Earth's surface to help them to locate places accurately.

Lines of latitude are circles drawn around the Earth parallel to the equator. Latitude is measured in degrees (°) north or south of the equator which is 0° latitude.

Lines of longitude, or meridians, run north-south between the Poles where they meet. They are measured in degrees east or west of the first, or prime meridian, which is 0° longitude. The prime meridian runs through Greenwich in England.

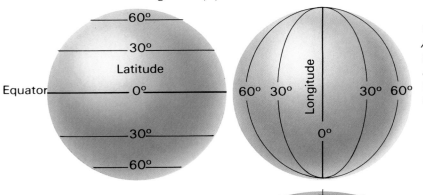

Compass points

A map is usually drawn so that north is at the top of the page. Sometimes the map will have a small arrow showing which direction north is. If you know where north is, you can tell in which direction south, west and east lie.

Latitude and longitude

The lines of latitude and longitude together form a grid or network of lines which make it possible to locate any place on the Earth's surface.

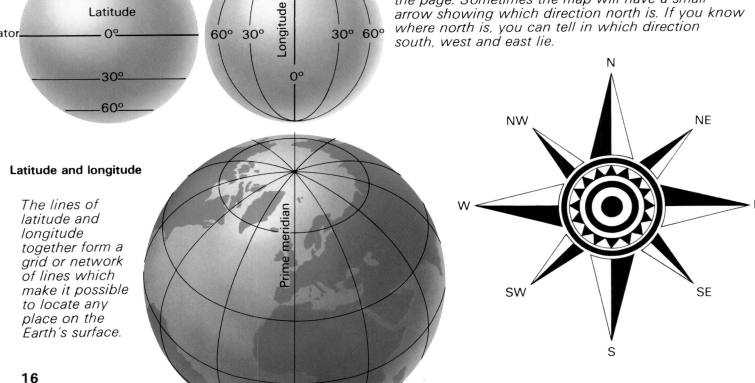

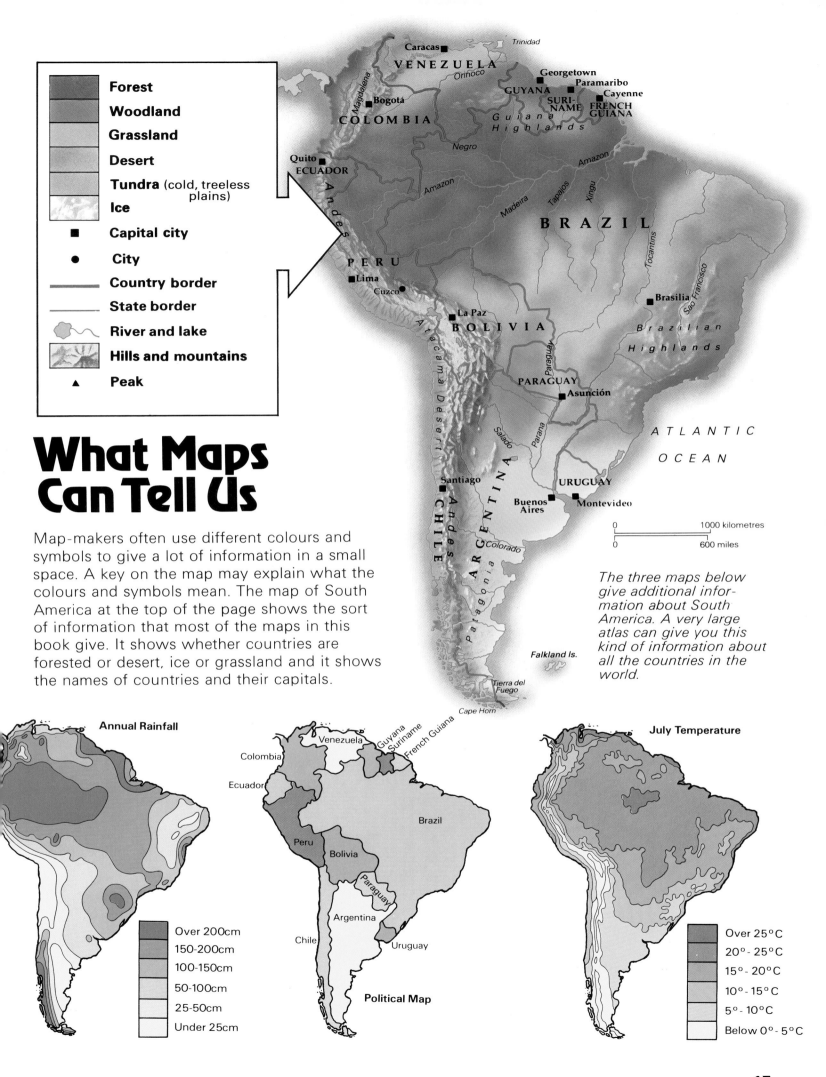

Key

Forest
Woodland
Grassland
Desert
Tundra (cold, treeless plains)
Ice
■ Capital city
● City
— Country border
— State border
River and lake
Hills and mountains
▲ Peak

What Maps Can Tell Us

Map-makers often use different colours and symbols to give a lot of information in a small space. A key on the map may explain what the colours and symbols mean. The map of South America at the top of the page shows the sort of information that most of the maps in this book give. It shows whether countries are forested or desert, ice or grassland and it shows the names of countries and their capitals.

The three maps below give additional information about South America. A very large atlas can give you this kind of information about all the countries in the world.

| 0 | 1000 kilometres |
| 0 | 600 miles |

Annual Rainfall

Over 200cm
150-200cm
100-150cm
50-100cm
25-50cm
Under 25cm

Political Map

July Temperature

Over 25°C
20°-25°C
15°-20°C
10°-15°C
5°-10°C
Below 0°-5°C

17

Left: *St. Peter's Square, Rome. Rome is the capital of Italy.*
Below: *The Arc de Triomphe, Paris. Paris is the capital of France.*

Fishing boat

Left: *The capital of Sweden, Stockholm, in winter.*

Europe

Europe is a small, densely populated continent divided into many different countries.

There are some very productive farming areas in Europe where the fertile land can be farmed intensively — which means a big yield can be obtained from a small area.

Maize is the main cereal grown in southern Europe but in northern France and Germany it is too cool for maize and so wheat is grown. Further north still, in Finland and Sweden, rye and barley are the main cereal crops. Vegetables are grown and dairy cattle kept near most big towns and cities to provide fresh food. Some areas, like Cornwall in England, southern Sweden and Denmark, are particularly important for dairy farming, while the warmer southern countries specialize in fruit growing.

However, in spite of the fertile land and mechanized farming methods in use in much of Europe, the continent is too small and highly populated to be completely self-supporting in food. To pay for the extra food brought in (imported), European countries sell abroad (export) a huge variety of manufactured goods.

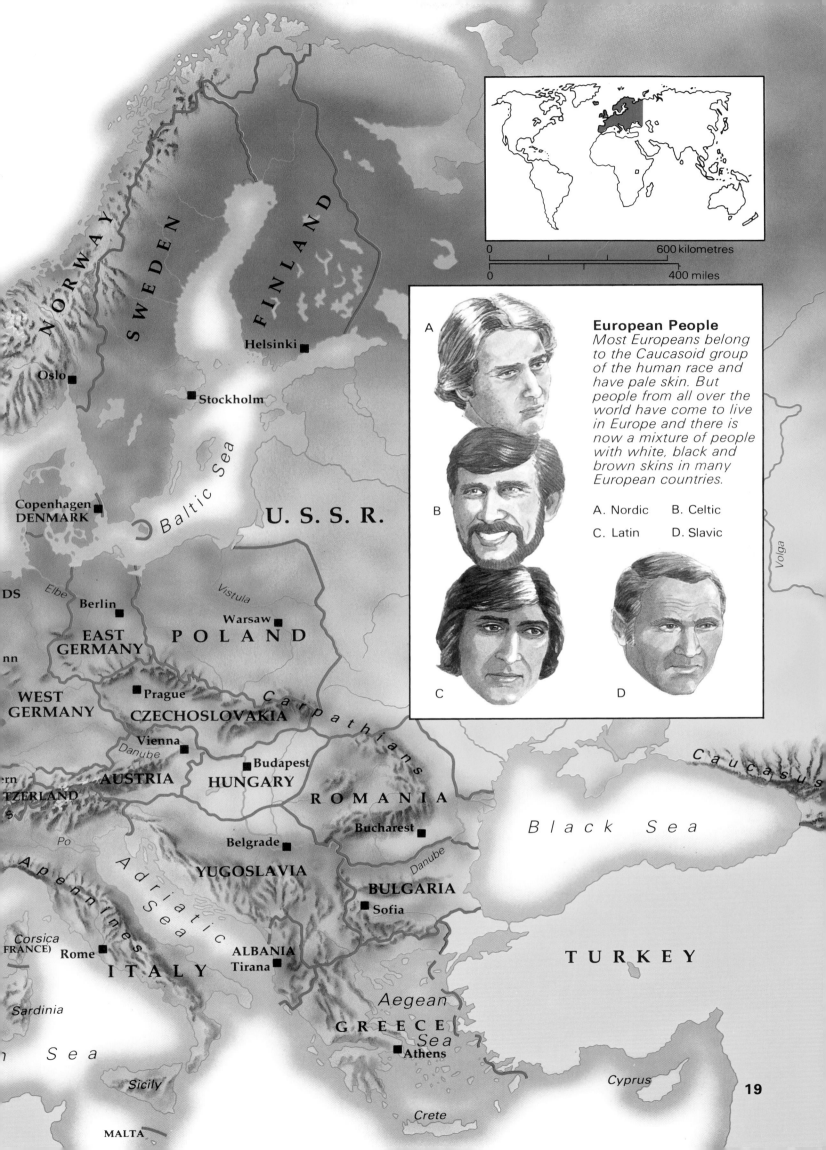

NORWAY

SWEDEN

FINLAND

Helsinki

Oslo

Stockholm

Baltic Sea

U.S.S.R.

Copenhagen
DENMARK

DS

Elbe

Berlin

Vistula

EAST
GERMANY

P O L A N D

Warsaw

WEST
GERMANY

Prague

Carpathians

nn

CZECHOSLOVAKIA

Vienna

Danube

AUSTRIA

Budapest

HUNGARY

R O M A N I A

TZERLAND

rn

Bucharest

Belgrade

Danube

Po

YUGOSLAVIA

Apennines

Adriatic Sea

BULGARIA

Sofia

Caucasus

Volga

Black Sea

Corsica
(FRANCE)

Rome

ALBANIA
Tirana

I T A L Y

Sardinia

Aegean

G R E E C E
Sea

Athens

T U R K E Y

Sea

Sicily

Cyprus

MALTA

Crete

European People

Most Europeans belong to the Caucasoid group of the human race and have pale skin. But people from all over the world have come to live in Europe and there is now a mixture of people with white, black and brown skins in many European countries.

A. Nordic   B. Celtic
C. Latin   D. Slavic

0   600 kilometres

0   400 miles

19

Among the most important industries in Europe are steel-making and the production of machinery, ships, cars, aeroplanes, lorries, buses, textiles, chemicals, processed foods, paper and pulp and many different kinds of consumer goods like televisions, cookers, washing machines, shoes and clothes.

Europe was the first part of the world to develop mechanized industries — in Britain, Belgium, France and Germany. Some of the major industrial regions of Europe are still in these countries, concentrated in coal producing areas. Industries originally developed in these places as the coal was needed to power the steam-driven machinery of the 18th century Industrial Revolution.

Above: *Tides can be used to create electrical power. On the River Rance in France the tide operates turbines in this dam.*

Coal is still an important source of energy in Europe, but now oil and natural gas are also used. Europe has its own deposits of oil and gas but still has to import a lot of oil so some countries are experimenting to see if nuclear power will supply their energy needs.

Communications are good in Europe with many surfaced roads and railway links. Rivers and canals are also important for transport.

The European Economic Community

In the past, European countries have fought many wars against each other. Now, many countries see their needs and aims as being the same. Ten countries — France, Italy, Belgium, W. Germany, Luxembourg, Netherlands, Denmark, Ireland, United Kingdom and Greece — are now joined together in the European Economic Community (E.E.C.) or Common Market. Spain and Portugal hope to join soon. This organization encourages member countries to trade with each other and to adopt common standards and laws.

Northern Europe

Norway, Sweden, Denmark, Finland and Iceland are in Northern Europe. Together, Norway, Sweden and Denmark are sometimes called Scandinavia.

Much of Norway, Sweden and Finland is covered in forests. Millions of coniferous trees are cut down every year and floated down rivers to the sawmills. Wood products, especially wood pulp for making newspaper, are very important exports, and lots of people work in the many industries which process the timber.

Finland is the land of a thousand lakes. They

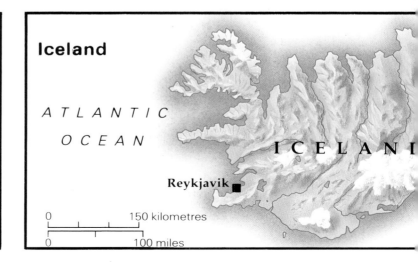

Iceland

ATLANTIC
OCEAN

ICELAND

Reykjavik ■

0   150 kilometres

0   100 miles

cover one-tenth of the country. Farming and forestry employ most of the people in Finland.

Southern Sweden and Denmark are quite different from the rest of this area. They are lowland regions where the forests have been cleared and the land is used for farming. Dairy cattle and pigs are kept and cheese, butter and bacon are exported. The farms are small and the farmers join together to sell their produce.

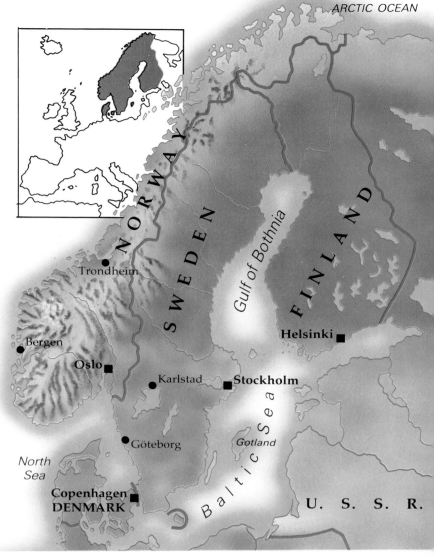

Left: *Norway's coastline is deeply indented with fjords cut by glaciers in the ice age. Norway is very mountainous and has a lot of snow in winter but her coastline is kept ice-free by a warm current.*

Below: *Logs being floated down to a sawmill in Sweden.*

Above: *A hydro-electric power station in Norway. Hydro-electricity is an important source of power in Northern Europe where there are waterfalls which can be harnessed to make electricity. Norway also has a new source of power and wealth in her North Sea oil fields.*

Iceland used to belong to Denmark but has been independent since 1944. Fishing is very important and the cod and herring Iceland's fishermen catch are canned or frozen in her processing factories. Fishing employs a lot of people throughout Northern Europe.

In the Netherlands more than half the population live on land reclaimed from the sea called polderland.

The Netherlands, Belgium and Luxembourg

These countries are all small and low-lying but they are highly populated, wealthy countries with some well-developed industries and very productive farms.

The Netherlands is often called Holland, though this name really only refers to the western, very low, part of the country. The Netherlands now has a very valuable source of power in the vast deposits of natural gas found near Groningen and under the North Sea. There are manufacturing industries producing beer, cheese, linen and sugar using materials produced in the country and a range of other industries using imported materials.

Above: *The cheese market in Alkmaar, Holland.*
Left: *Rotterdam is a very large port. Situated at the mouth of the Rhine, it is used by many barges carrying cargoes to and from Switzerland, France and West Germany.*

Belgium has some large deposits of coal and these have helped Belgian industries to grow. The northern half of Belgium is low-lying with very rich agricultural land used to grow wheat, sugar beet, vegetables and flax. The flax is used to weave linen.

Luxembourg is a small, land-locked country. Deposits of iron ore in the south led to iron, steel and metal-working industries being established. A quarter of the population works in farming with barley, oats, potatoes, sugar beet and wheat the main crops.

The British Isles

The British Isles includes England, Scotland, Wales, Northern Ireland and the Irish Republic as well as the Channel Islands and the Isle of Man. The United Kingdom is England, Scotland, Wales and Northern Ireland. Great Britain means England, Scotland and Wales.

Britain has large deposits of coal and iron ore and was one of the first places in the world to develop steam-power and mechanized industries. Britain is still an important manufacturing nation, producing a wide variety of goods and machinery, but now, the cost of importing raw materials and fuels, and the growth of industries in other countries, means the British Isles are less wealthy.

Britain must export enough manufactured goods to pay for the food she needs to import. Although her farms are very efficient and highly mechanized they are just not big enough to produce more than 60% of the food needed by the large population.

Red deer

Fox

Rabbit

Otter

Badger

Left: *Nelson's Column in Trafalgar Square, London. London is the capital of England.*

Above: *A small farm on the Isle of Skye in Scotland where the fields are too small to use much machinery.*

23

Above: *Steel works in Port Talbot, Wales.*

Right: *The Sullom Voe oil terminal in the Shetland Islands, Scotland. The discovery of oil and gas under the North Sea in the 1970s has brought wealth to Britain.*

Above: *There are many different kinds of houses throughout the British Isles.*

Above: *Although there are a great many people living in England and a great many cities, towns and roads have been built, there is still a good deal of beautiful countryside and rich farmland.*

Left: *Fishing is important off the coast of the British Isles. Here the trawlermen are sorting their catch.*

Right: *The Giant's Causeway in Northern Ireland.*

Orkney
Islands

*North West
Highlands*

Inverness

Hebrides

Aberdeen
Dee

Tay

Grampians

SCOTLAND

Edinburgh

Glasgow *Clyde*

**North Sea
oil rig**

Newcastle
Tyne

A *T L A N T I C*

O C E A N

**NORTHERN
IRELAND**

Belfast

Isle of Man

Pennines

*Irish
Sea*

REPUBLIC

O F

IRELAND

Leeds Hull

*North
Sea*

Liverpool

Manchester

Shannon

Trent

ENGLAND

Norwich

Dublin

WALES *Cambrian Mts.*

Birmingham *Ouse*

Cork

Severn

Avon

Swansea

London

Thames

Cardiff

Dover

Southampton

Plymouth

Isle of Wight

Isles of Scilly

E n g l i s h   C h a n n e l

0   200 kilometres

0   100 miles

Channel Is.

FRANCE

France and Southern Europe

Farming is very important in France. The fact that the climate of France varies so much from the cool, moist north to the warm, Mediterranean south, means that many different crops can be grown. These include barley, flax, oats, sugar beet, wheat, apples, grapes, peaches and apricots. Livestock are kept and dairy farming is particularly important: France produces over 300 different types of cheese!

Alongside her farms, France has thriving industries producing chemicals, iron and steel goods, cars and textiles. Hydro-electric and nuclear energy help power French industry and France also has rich reserves of iron ore.

The countries of southern Europe — Portugal, Spain, Italy, Greece (and southern France) — have

Cross-Channel hovercraft

Calais
Boulogne
BELGIUM
WEST
Dieppe
Le Havre
Brest
Seine
Paris
Strasbourg
Loire
Tours
F R A N C E
Dijon
Saône

Bay of Biscay
Bordeaux
Dordogne
Lyon
Garonne
C e n t r a l
Bilbao
M a s s i f
Rhône
Grenoble
Turi
Oporto
Duero
Toulouse
P y r e n e e s
Avignon
Alps
Pamplona
ANDORRA
Ebro
Marseille
Nice
MONA
Tagus
Lisbon
Madrid
S P A I N
Corsica
(FRANCE)
Guadiana
Barcelona
P O R T U G A L
Seville
B a l e a r i c   I s.
(SPAIN)
Minorca
Sardinia
(ITALY)
Segura
Ibiza
Majorca
Alicante
Malaga
Gibraltar
(U.K.)
M e a

0		500 kilometres
0		300 miles

Left: *Grapes are grown, to make wine, all over Southern Europe.*

Right: *The olive tree's long roots help it to live in a dry climate. It gives oil and wood as well as olives.*

hot, dry summers ideal for ripening cereals and fruit. Barley and wheat will grow in the mild, wet winters and then ripen early in the summer. Grapes, oranges and lemons also ripen well and the hot summers dry the grapes to make raisins and currants.

Italy is the most highly industrialized of the southern European lands, having large car and chemical producing plants. Greece, Spain and Portugal are still mainly agricultural nations with no great wealth as the dry land is unsuitable for intensive farming methods.

Right: *The hot, dry weather in Southern Europe attracts many tourists.*
Below: *Venice, in Italy, is well known for its canals and gondolas.*

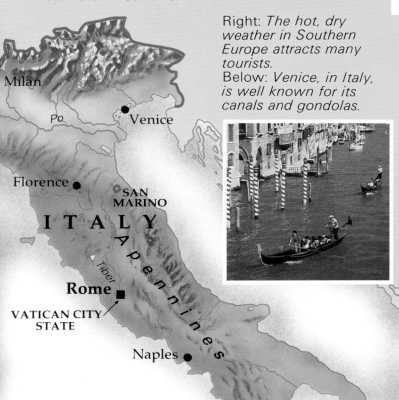

Milan

Po

Venice

Florence

SAN MARINO

ITALY

Apennines

Tiber

Rome

VATICAN CITY STATE

Naples

Sicily

rranean

Sea

MALTA

Thessaloniki

Pindus Mts.

Aegean

GREECE

Sea

Athens

Crete

Above: *Winter sports attract many visitors to Austria, Switzerland and Northern Italy.*

Left: *The Rhine flows right through Germany to Switzerland and gives Switzerland an outlet to the sea as barges can be towed as far as Basel.*

Germany, Austria and Switzerland

Germany is divided into two parts : West Germany, which is properly called the Federal Republic of Germany, and East Germany or the German Democratic Republic.

West Germany is a very rich industrial nation. Agriculture is important too, with dairy and fruit farming in the north-west and the fertile lands of central and southern Germany producing rich crops of wheat, oats, barley, maize, sugar beet and potatoes. Famous wines come from the Rhine and Mosel valleys.

East Germany has some rich farmland but had few industries before the Second World War. Since then great efforts have been made by the communist government to start new ones. There are rich fields of lignite — a type of coal — which can be used to heat homes and fuel power stations. Like coal, it can also be used as the raw material in the manufacture of synthetic fibres and some chemicals.

Much of Austria is covered by the Alps, and winter sports bring many tourists. Timber and timber products are important and Austria is also rich in iron ore. Great use is made of hydro-electric power in Austria and in Switzerland.

Switzerland, like Austria, has no coastline, and is very mountainous. Tourism is important but the Swiss also have many industries producing a variety of goods, including scientific instruments, electrical equipment, watches, textiles, paper and chocolate.

Above: *In the summer cattle are driven up to the high pastures in the Alps. The cows wear bells so they can be found easily.*

Right: *The beautiful city of Vienna is the capital of Austria.*

28

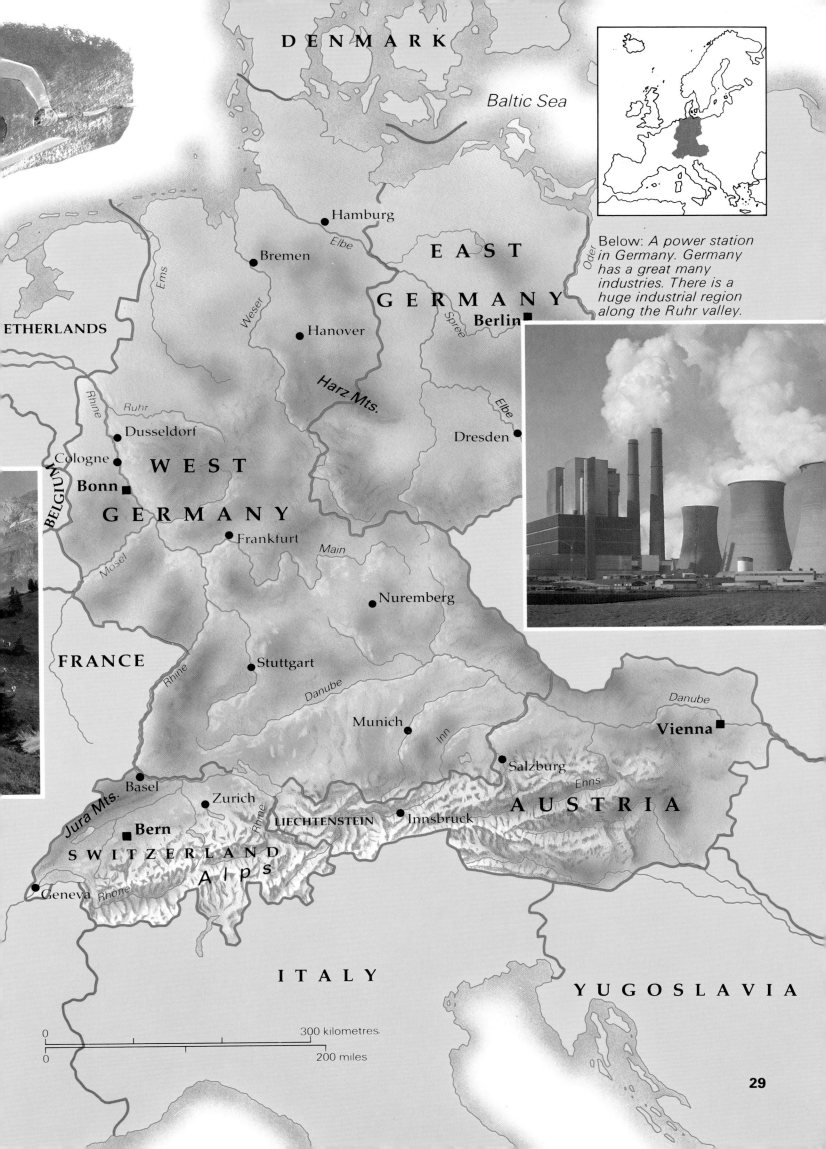

D E N M A R K

Baltic Sea

E A S T

G E R M A N Y

Hamburg

Elbe

Bremen

Oder

Weser

Berlin

Hanover

Spree

Ems

ETHERLANDS

Rhine

Ruhr

Elbe

Dusseldorf

W E S T

Dresden

Cologne

BELGIUM

Bonn

G E R M A N Y

Harz Mts.

Frankfurt

Main

Mosel

Nuremberg

FRANCE

Rhine

Stuttgart

Danube

Danube

Munich

Inn

Vienna

Salzburg

Enns

Basel

Zurich

Rhine

A U S T R I A

Jura Mts.

LIECHTENSTEIN

Innsbruck

Bern

S W I T Z E R L A N D

Alps

Geneva *Rhone*

I T A L Y

Y U G O S L A V I A

Below: *A power station in Germany. Germany has a great many industries. There is a huge industrial region along the Ruhr valley.*

0 _____ 300 kilometres
0 _____ 200 miles

29

Central and Eastern Europe

Poland, Czechoslovakia, Hungary, Yugoslavia, Albania, Romania and Bulgaria are all communist countries which means most of their industries, mines and farms are run by the government.

Poland is low-lying and cooler in the north and more rugged and warmer in the south. There are rich deposits of coal and copper in Poland and industries include textiles, chemicals, iron and steel, ship-building, paper, shoes and cars. Another important industry is food processing: Poland has some rich agricultural lands producing rye, wheat and sugar beet.

Hungary is a vast plain surrounded by mountains. Farming is very important and, as well as cereal and livestock farming, there are vineyards. Hungary mines lignite, coal, iron and bauxite (from which aluminium can be made) and has industries to process these raw materials.

Czechoslovakia has two distinct groups of people — the Czechs and the Slovaks. They each speak a different language. The country has rich deposits of coal and gets oil by pipeline from the U.S.S.R.

Unlike the other countries in this region, Yugoslavia has a large tourist industry, with many holiday-makers coming to her warm Adriatic coast. Cereals like maize and wheat can be grown in the Danube basin and grapes and sugar beet on the plains and lower slopes of the mountains. Minerals are plentiful and several hydro-electric power schemes have been set up.

Above: *Roses are grown in Bulgaria for making perfume.*

Above left: *Although Poland is making great efforts to modernize her farms, there is still a lack of new machinery.*

Left: *Barges on the River Danube are an important means of transport and a great variety of goods are carried.*

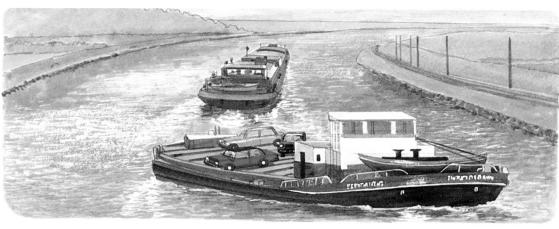

Albania has only recently begun to develop industries and modernize her farms. The rich forests in the mountainous regions provide timber and on the lower slopes there is grazing for sheep and goats and fertile farm land. Albania has deposits of coal, copper and some oil.

Romania has very varied scenery including high mountains, fertile valleys, plains, hills, and the marshy delta region of the Danube. There are many farms but a lack of rain means

Romania is not a major food producer. There are oil refineries to process Romania's own oil and there are also supplies of natural gas but the country has few other minerals.

Bulgaria is also lacking in mineral wealth and this lack of raw materials has held up industrial growth. But like many countries in this area, Bulgaria receives help from the U.S.S.R. in the shape of oil and other raw materials. Crops grown for export include cotton, roses (for perfume), fruit and tobacco.

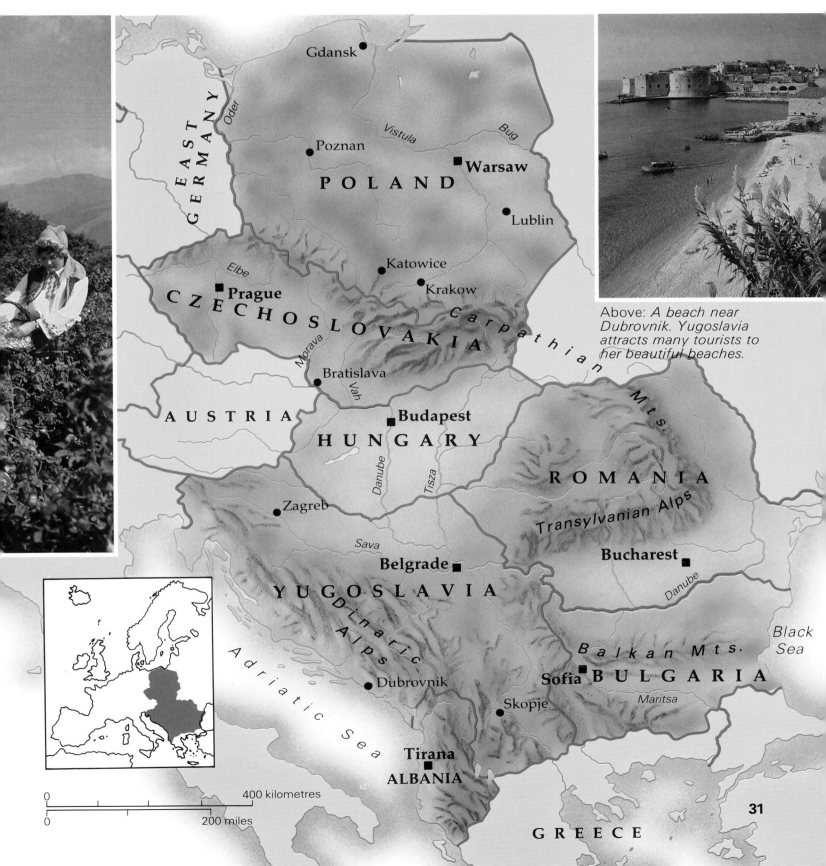

Above: *A beach near Dubrovnik. Yugoslavia attracts many tourists to her beautiful beaches.*

0
400 kilometres
0
200 miles

Above: *Samarkand is in the south of the U.S.S.R.*

Left: *Red Square in Moscow, the capital of the U.S.S.R.*

U.S.S.R.

The Union of Soviet Socialist Republics (U.S.S.R.) is the largest country in the world. It is the union of 15 different republics each of which has its own government for domestic matters.

Until this century the U.S.S.R. had few industries and her farms were not modernized. After the communists came to power in 1917 they made great efforts to change this and now the U.S.S.R. is a leading producer of many different products and goods.

The U.S.S.R. has huge deposits of coal, oil and natural gas, as well as hydro-electric power to fuel her industries. Among her many

Brown bear

Wolf

Reindeer

mineral deposits are vast reserves of iron ore, copper and asbestos.

Not all of the U.S.S.R. is equally advanced. European Russia, the area west of the Ural Mountains, is the most highly populated and developed part of the country. The southern part of European Russia is the Russian Steppes which is a very rich farming area. Wheat, maize and other crops are grown in large quantities.

To the east of the Ural Mountains is the vast region known as Siberia. Most of Siberia is very sparsely populated and very cold. South of Siberia lie the Southern Asiatic Republics. These are mainly desert areas with some oases which are fed by the rivers draining from the Pamirs and other high mountain ranges. Cotton and many fruits are grown.

Above: *The northern part of Siberia is a very cold, bare region where only mosses and lichens grow. But valuable minerals, including gold and diamonds, have been found there so efforts are being made to improve communications.*

Asia

Asia is the largest continent and is home for more than half the people in the world. This huge region has many varied landscapes. In the Tien Shan, Pamir and Hindu Kush mountain ranges there are peaks reaching over 6 000 metres, and in the Himalayas are the two tallest mountains in the world — K2 (8 611 metres) and Everest (8 848 metres). These mountainous regions are not the only cold areas in Asia; there are cold lowlands too, especially in Siberia.

Asia also has very hot regions, some of which are dry, desert lands while others are wet and forested. The deserts of Asia stretch across the Middle East and southern U.S.S.R. into the Gobi desert of northern China. There is also a desert region in north-west India and in Pakistan.

There are forests in other parts of India and over much of South-East Asia. These areas have a monsoon climate which means that there is rain in summer but the winters are dry. In very wet areas the undergrowth beneath the trees grows very thick making dense jungle.

In many parts of Asia the people live by farming and can only grow enough to feed themselves. This is called subsistence farming and if the crops are poor then people go hungry. The most popular crop is rice which grows especially well in the river valleys. In the deserts there are nomads and small communities gathered around oases just as there are in the Sahara desert in Africa. In other parts of Asia there are plantations which grow crops for sale. This is known as commercial farming. There are tea plantations in India and Sri Lanka and rubber plantations in Malaysia.

The number of industries in Asia is growing: U.S.S.R., India and China all have large programmes to expand their industries and Japan is already one of the most highly industrialized nations in the world. There are many valuable natural resources in Asia, including oil in the Middle East, many different minerals in India, China and the U.S.S.R. and tin in Malaysia and Thailand.

Right: *Singapore is made up of Singapore Island and 60 smaller islands. It is a major port.*

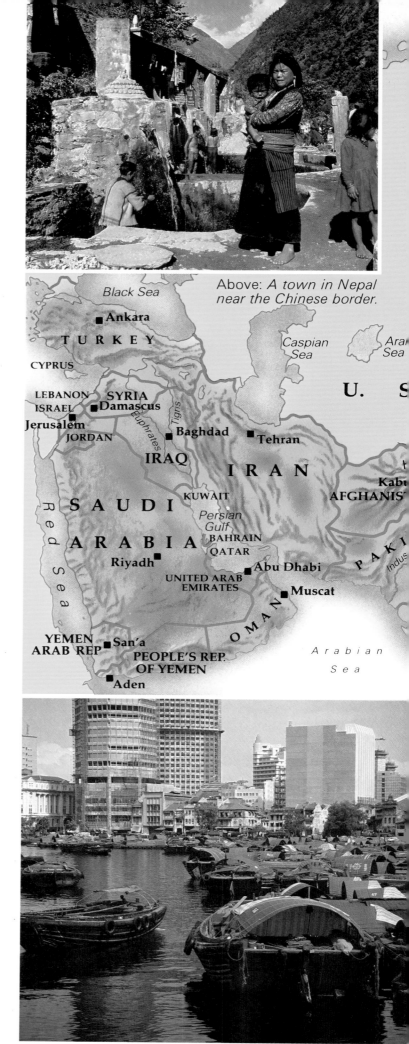

Above: *A town in Nepal near the Chinese border.*

Left: *A Buddhist monk in a temple in Thailand. The religion of Buddhism was founded in India but there are now over 220 million Buddhists spread throughout the world.*

S i b e r i a

Ulan Bator

M O N G O L I A

G o b i   D e s e r t

R. *Tien Shan*

Amur

NORTH
KOREA

Pyongyang

Peking

Hwang Ho

Seoul

SOUTH
KOREA

J A P A N

Tokyo

P A C I F I C

O C E A N

C H I N A

irs

K2 ▲

abad

Indus

Himalayas

T I B E T

**New
Delhi**

NEPAL Everest ▲

Katmandu **BHUTAN**

Ganges

BANGLADESH

Dacca

I N D I A

Yangtze Kiang

Si Kiang

Taipei

TAIWAN

HONG
KONG

BURMA

Irrawaddy

Hanoi

LAOS

VIETNAM

Vientiane

Mekong

S o u t h

Manila

PHILIPPINES

Rangoon

THAILAND

Bangkok

KAMPUCHEA

**Phnom
Penh**

C h i n a

S e a

*B a y   o f
B e n g a l*

Above: *The Chinese people belong to the Mongoloid group of the human race and have yellowish skin and straight black hair.*

BRUNEI

**SRI
LANKA**

Colombo

N D I A N   O C E A N

M A L A Y S I A

**Kuala
Lumpur**

SINGAPORE

I N D O N E S I A

Jakarta

0   1000 kilometres

0   600 miles

Note: *Turkey and the U.S.S.R. are partly in Asia and partly in Europe.*

The Middle East

The Middle East is the area south of the U.S.S.R. and east of the Mediterranean. Much of this region is covered by the dry, desert lands of Saudi Arabia, Iraq and Iran. They were once poor, but now they, and some of the smaller states along the Persian Gulf such as Kuwait and Bahrain, are very rich oil states. Pipelines carry oil from wells in the deserts to ports and refineries.

There is a lot more rain in the countries around the Mediterranean than in the dry oil states. Crops like wheat, barley, tobacco and fruit can be grown and agriculture is important in the Lebanon, Syria, Jordan and Turkey although manufacturing is now growing in importance in these regions.

Israel came into being in 1948 to provide a homeland for the Jewish people. The country lacks resources but the extensive use of irrigation means that lots of crops can be grown on the communal farms called kibbutzim. Citrus fruits and wine are important exports. A wide range of products are manufactured, processed or finished in Israel.

Afghanistan is a very mountainous country with no coastline. There are villages in the valleys where crops are grown and herds of sheep, horses, donkeys and camels are moved into the higher grazing lands in the summer.

Above: *Most people who live in this region are Muslims following the Islamic religion. Their god, Allah, is worshipped in mosques like this one.*

Above: *Oil wells and pipelines in Southern Iran. The oil states are using some of their wealth to experiment with ways of farming their infertile, desert lands.*

Above: *A kibbutz in Israel.*

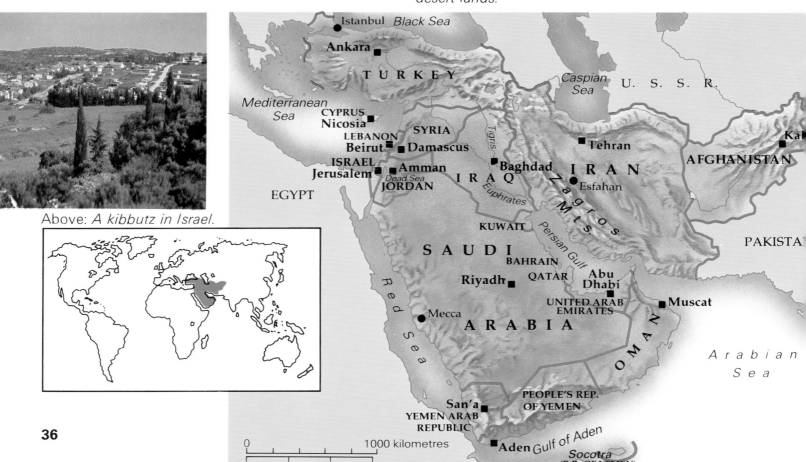

U.S.S.R.

MONGOLIA

Altai Mts.

Tien Shan

Tarim

Ulan Bator

Gobi Desert

Peking

Pyongyang

NORTH KOREA

Seoul

SOUTH KOREA

Amur

TIBET

Lhasa

Tsang Po

NEPAL

Himalayas

CHINA

Sian

Hwang Ho

Shanghai

Yangtze Kiang

Mekong

Si-Kiang

Kwangchow (Canton)

HONG KONG

Taipei

TAIWAN

VIETNAM

0   1000 kilometres
0   600 miles

Above: *These people are Mongols. Mongolia was a Chinese province until 1911 but it is now independent.*

Below: *A street scene in China.*

Above: *Seoul, the capital of South Korea. North and South Korea used to be one country.*

China and her Neighbours

China is one of the largest countries in the world and is home for nearly one quarter of the world's population. Much of China is covered in high mountains and the north-west is desert, so most of China's people live in the east — on the lower ground around the coast or in the river valleys.

In the rich soils of the river valleys, where floods deposit fresh silt every year, rice is the major food crop and cotton is also grown. Tea is grown on terraced hillsides in the south. Fishing is an important source of food around the coast.

After the Communists came to power in 1949 China began a great programme of modernization and dams, railways and factories were built. China has coal, lignite, oil

Below: *A Hong Kong junk. Hong Kong has a very busy port and many industries. The junks are used for fishing, carrying cargoes and as homes.*

and hydro-electric power to fuel her industries and many rich mineral deposits.

Taiwan is an island which used to be known as Formosa. Exiles from mainland China settled here after 1949.

Japan

Japan consists of four main islands — Hokkaido, Honshu, Shikoku and Kyushu — and hundreds of other tiny islands. Most of the land is mountainous. The small amount of low land is intensively farmed. Rice is the main food crop and fruit is grown in many places. Tea and mulberry bushes (the leaves are used to feed silk worms) are grown on the hillsides, many of which are forested and are a useful source of timber. Fishing is a very important industry in Japan.

Japan is not rich in natural resources, but is still a very rich manufacturing nation, importing raw materials (such as iron ore from Australia and oil from the Middle East), and exporting a huge variety of manufactured goods including ships, trucks, cars, motorbikes all sorts of electronic and telecommunications equipment, man-made fibres, cameras, cement, steel, cigarettes and watches.

Above: *A Shinto festival. Shinto and Buddhism are the main religions in Japan.*
Below: *Mount Fujiyama, the highest mountain in Japan, is an extinct volcano. There are about 140 extinct and 60 active volcanos in Japan.*

Above: *Tokyo, the capital of Japan, is a very busy and crowded city. The shortage of flat land is so serious in Japan that many of the newest industries have been set up on land reclaimed from the sea.*

Hokkaido
• Sapporo

• Sendai

PACIFIC OCEAN

Sea of Japan

H o n s h u

■ **Tokyo**
Fujiyama ▲ • Yokohama

Kyoto •
Kobe • • Osaka
• Hamamatsu

Hiroshima •

Kitakyushu •

Shikoku

Nagasaki •

Kyushu

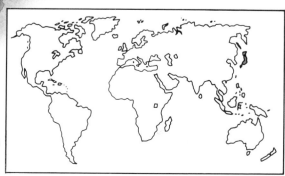

0
0
300 kilometres
200 miles

Right: *Rice terraces in the Philippines.*

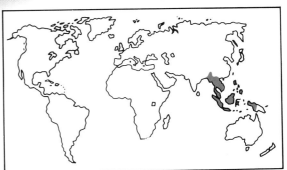

South-East Asia

South-East Asia includes Burma, Thailand, Malaysia, Singapore, Laos, Vietnam, Kampuchea, Indonesia and the Philippines.

These countries all have some high mountains and dense forest regions and receive heavy monsoon rainfall for part of the year. In the lowlands, such as the Irrawaddy valley and delta in Burma and the Mekong river and delta in Vietnam, rice growing is very important. As well as the food crops grown for local needs, there are also some cash crops grown for export, including coffee, tobacco and rubber. These crops are often grown on large plantations.

Indonesia is a collection of over 3 000 islands. Java is the most important island as it is where over half the population of Indonesia lives and where most of the commercial farming takes place. Indonesia has some rich oil deposits.

North of Indonesia lie the many islands of the Philippines — over 7 000 in all. The islands are very mountainous and have some active volcanos, as do the islands of Indonesia.

Right: *Tin mining in Malaysia. Malaysia is one of the few countries in the world which has deposits of tin — a very valuable mineral. Here tin is being dredged up from the river bed.*

Stilt-house in Thailand

U.S.S.R.

| 0 | 600 kilometres |
| 0 | 400 miles |

AFGHANISTAN

Hindu Kush

Indus

Islamabad

IRAN

PAKISTAN

Indus

Karachi

Thar Desert

New Delhi

Himalayas

CHINA

NEPAL
Katmandu

Mount Everest

BHUTAN

Darjeeling

Brahmaputra

INDIA

Ganges

BANGLADESH
Dacca

Calcutta

Chittagong

BURM

Mahanadi

Tiger

Bombay

Godavari

Ghats

Indian elephant

Western Ghats

Hyderabad

Krishna

Eastern Ghats

Madras

Bay of Bengal

Right: *Floods after monsoon rains in Bangladesh.*

SRI LANKA
Colombo

India and her Neighbours

This area is often called Southern Asia and includes Pakistan, India, Bangladesh and the island of Sri Lanka.

Rice is the most important crop in this region. In the drier areas millet is grown as well as wheat, chickpeas, groundnuts (peanuts) and sugar-cane. Farming is still very primitive with few machines and a great shortage of fertilizers. Often, not enough is grown to support the farmers themselves. There are, however, a few crops grown for sale: tea is an important export for India and Sri Lanka and cotton and jute are grown and processed in parts of India, Bangladesh and Pakistan.

Pakistan is a very dry land but it is crossed

40

by the River Indus which is the lifeline of the country. It provides water for the towns, irrigation for the crops and also hydro-electric power. Pakistan has some industries including textiles, food processing and chemicals.

Farming throughout India depends on the monsoon rainfall which comes in the summer. The coastal areas receive a great deal of rain in the wet season, but the inland areas may receive much less and the amount varies from year to year. If there is too little rain the crops won't grow. Too much rain can wash the crops out of the ground. India has deposits of oil, coal, iron ore, manganese, copper and bauxite and has a variety of industries.

Bangladesh is situated in the low-lying lands of the Ganges delta and here the rain is so heavy and the river so high, that floods are very common in the summer. In the autumn tropical cyclones can bring more floods from the Bay of Bengal. The people are mostly very poor and industries are few.

Sri Lanka has high mountains in the middle and here tea is grown. The lowlands all around are suitable for rice, with coconuts growing near the coast. Coconuts give oil, food and matting from the hair on the shell.

Below: *High up in the kingdom of Nepal, where it is very cold, the people use yaks to carry loads and to plough.*

Above: *Hinduism is the traditional religion of India. Hindus believe that the River Ganges is the earthly form of the Goddess Ganga and pilgrims come to bathe in the river.*

Above right: *Although more factories are being built in this region, traditional crafts are still practised widely.*

Left: *A farmer ploughing in the Brahmaputra River valley.*

Right: *Fishermen in the south of India. The sail on one of the boats has been carefully made by stitching together old sacks.*

Africa

Africa is a huge continent with an enormous variety of climates, landscapes and peoples. It does not have such a big population as Europe or Asia, but as a lot of Africa is covered by desert or by dense forest, the more fertile regions are well-populated and a shortage of food is a real problem in some countries.

Africa is the home of very many different groups of people. Arabs and Berbers live in the north, while south of the Sahara desert there are very many different black African tribes speaking over 1000 different languages. In addition, many Europeans have made their home in Africa.

Until the 19th century, the rest of the world knew very little about the centre of Africa and called it the 'dark continent' because of this, although North Africa and the coastal regions were known to Europeans centuries before. From the 16th century right up to the

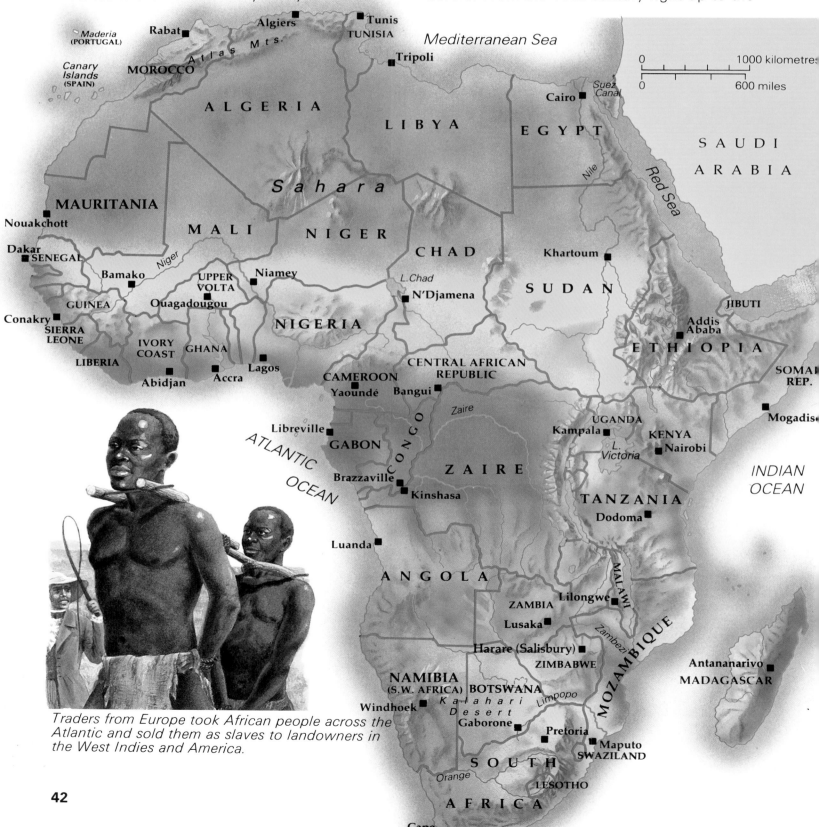

Traders from Europe took African people across the Atlantic and sold them as slaves to landowners in the West Indies and America.

middle of the 19th, European traders practised a cruel trade in people — taking black Africans from the coastal regions to work as slaves on the great plantations in America and the West Indies.

In the 19th century, as explorers began to penetrate the mysterious interior, many European countries began to extend their interests in Africa, dividing the countries south of the Sahara between them. The countries ruled by European powers were called colonies and Belgium, Britain, France, Germany, Italy, Portugal and Spain all had colonies in Africa. Now most of Africa is independent, although the new nations have many problems to overcome with widespread poverty and lack of education among their people. Progress is being made, however, as countries discover and develop their valuable mineral resources, start new industries and make agriculture more efficient and productive.

Above: *Nomads in South Morocco. They ride the camels perched right on top of the camel's hump.*

Below: *Cape Town, in South Africa, lies at the foot of the appropriately named Table Mountain.*

Above: *A small village in Cameroon, West Africa.*

Right: *Henry Morton Stanley who, in the 1870s, led an expedition into East Africa in search of the famous explorer David Livingstone.*

Right: *The modern city of Lagos which is the capital of Nigeria. Industries in Lagos include ship repairing and textiles.*

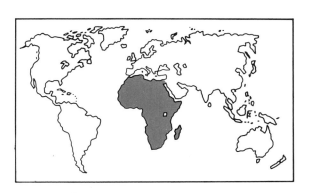

Northern Africa

Africa has a climate and landscape like Mediterranean Europe along the north coast of Morocco, Algeria and Tunisia. Along this coastline oranges, lemons, peaches, apricots, grapes, dates and olive trees are grown. Goats and sheep are kept as they can manage to find a little food even in the hot, dry summers and, wherever possible, irrigation schemes have been started to help farmers.

South of this more fertile region stretches the vast Sahara desert. Very hot by day and very cold at night, the desert has few inhabitants. The people who do live there are either nomads, who move from place to place with their camels, sheep and horses, or people living in small settlements where there is a source of water. Some of these oases are very small, but others may have several thousand inhabitants. Date palms grow in the oases and the larger oases have fields of fruit, cereals and vegetables. Even the dry wastes of the desert contain some wealth. In Libya and Algeria large quantities of oil and natural gas have been discovered.

These nomads of the Sahara live in tents which they carry with them.

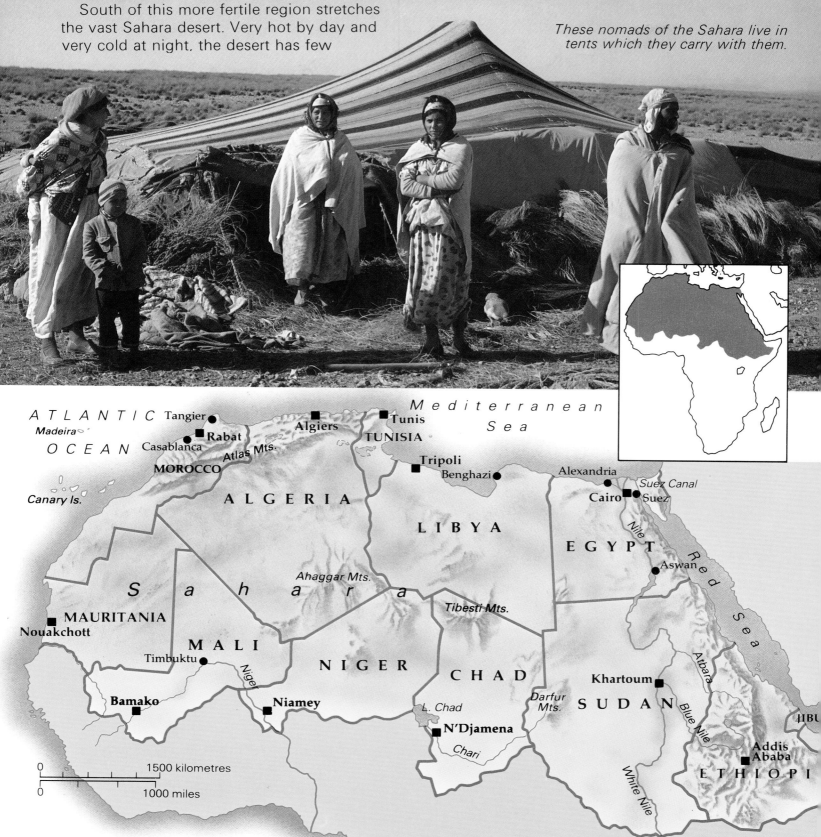

Above: *Date palms are very useful as they give dates for food, the leaves can be woven into mats and baskets, the stems can be used to make fences and ropes and the trunks provide wood for fuel.*

Above: *In Egypt the River Nile creates one great oasis which runs the length of the country. Most of Egypt's population live in this fertile valley. Huge dams have been built to store and control the water and to provide hydro-electric power.*

The Savanna

The Sahara gradually gives way to a great area of open grassland called savanna. In some parts of the savanna enough rain falls for crops like cotton, groundnuts (peanuts), maize, tobacco and even rice to grow. But in many parts the rainfall is unreliable and when crops fail famine can follow.

The savanna is home to a number of African tribes who herd cattle on the grasslands. They live in small communities in villages of grass or mud huts. Many animals live on the savanna.

Below: *The Masai people of East Africa live by herding their cattle on the savanna grasslands.*

Giraffe

Buffalo

Impala

Cheetah

Rhinoceros

Zebra

Lion

Middle Africa

Around the west coast of Africa it is wet and humid and some areas are covered in rainforests and swamps. The countries clustered around the west coast are changing rapidly, with new towns, industries and agricultural methods developing alongside simple farming communities. Wealth has come to this area from the discovery of many valuable minerals.

Nigeria is perhaps the richest country in West Africa, with large deposits of oil and coal as well as tin. Dams on the River Niger provide cheap hydro-electricity. Nigeria has around 250 different groups of people speaking different languages. The largest groups are the Hausa, Fulani, Yoruba and Ibo.

Inland, in the centre of Africa, lie the great tropical rainforests of the Zaire basin. Small tribes still live in the forests, making clearings to grow yams, sweet potatoes and bananas, and moving on when the soil is exhausted.

In the east are the mountainous regions of Ethiopia and the high, flat plateau lands of Uganda, Kenya and Tanzania. The grasslands here are called scrub or bush and crops include cotton, coffee, sisal, tea and maize. Cattle, sheep and goats are also kept. Valuable minerals have been discovered in Tanzania, including diamonds, lead, gold, tin and coal.

Hausa **Fulani** **Ibo**

Above: *Small tribes of pygmies live deep in the forest. The men hunt with bows and poison-tipped arrows.*

Above: *Panning for diamonds in Sierra Leone.*

46

Southern Africa

South of the forests of the Zaire basin is another stretch of grassland where cattle are kept and a variety of crops grown. Coffee is the main crop in Angola and maize and tobacco are grown in Zambia and Zimbabwe.

This region is rich in minerals with diamonds and iron in Angola, huge deposits of copper in Zambia and coal in Zimbabwe. Botswana has swamps in the north where nickel and copper have been found and also has reserves of coal and diamonds.

South Africa is a very rich country with vast

Above left: *The Zulus are traditionally great warriors. They make up about 25% of all the black people in South Africa. Most Zulus now live in towns.*

Above: *A diamond mine in South Africa.*

mineral resources. Oranges, apples, grapes, bananas, pineapples, sugar-cane and wheat all grow in the coastal regions. Inland it is much drier and irrigation schemes have been started wherever possible. On the high grasslands of South Africa, called the veld, cattle and sheep are kept and cotton and tobacco grown where there is enough rain.

South Africa has used some of the money earned from her vast deposits of gold and diamonds to start up industries.

Above: *The Kalahari desert is the home of the Kalahari Bushmen who live by hunting and gathering roots and berries.*

Grain stores on the prairies in Alberta, Canada.

North America

The major part of the continent of North America is divided into two very large countries — Canada and the United States of America (U.S.A.) Canada has 10 provinces and two territories. The U.S.A. is a union of 50 states, 48 of which are grouped together in the southern half of the continent. The 49th state is Alaska, which the U.S.A. bought from Russia in 1867, and the 50th is the Hawaiian islands in the Pacific Ocean.

North America has an enormous variety of landscapes and climates, ranging from the icy wastes of the Arctic Circle in northern Canada to the warm sub-tropical beaches of Florida. There are huge areas of fertile farmland. Between the Rockies and the Appalachian Mountains there are wide plains, drained by the river Mississippi and its tributaries, where fields stretch as far as the eye can see. In Canada the huge plains, called the prairies, have enormous fields too, which means very large machines can be used to harvest crops quickly and cheaply.

The people of North America have come to live there from all over the world. When European explorers reached the continent in

Above: *The vast ranges of the Rocky Mountains stretch from Alaska to California. For much of their length the Rockies run in two great chains: one chain down the Pacific coast, the other hundreds of kilometres inland.*

the 15th and 16th century, they found tribes of 'Red' Indians who had come from Siberia through Alaska more than 20 000 years before. Along the northern shores and offshore islands there were small groups of Eskimos.

The 13 states on the east coast of the U.S.A. were originally settled mainly by people from Britain. At first Britain treated these states as one of her colonies but the U.S.A. achieved independence in 1776. The early settlers brought Negroes from West Africa to work as slaves in the huge, hot plantations of the south. Slavery ended after the civil war between the northern and southern states in the 1860s.

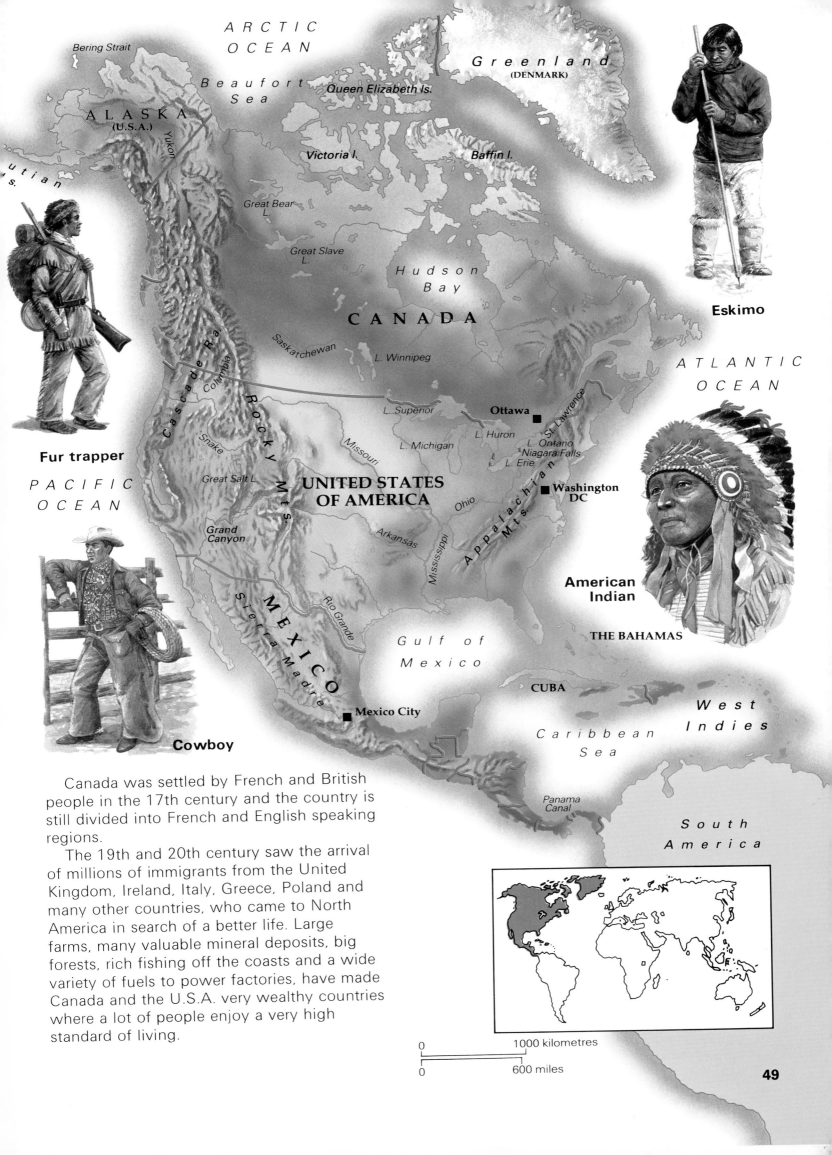

ARCTIC
OCEAN

Bering Strait

*Beaufort
Sea*

ALASKA
(U.S.A.)

Yukon

G r e e n l a n d
(DENMARK)

Queen Elizabeth Is.

Victoria I.

Baffin I.

*Great Bear
L.*

*Great Slave
L.*

*Hudson
Bay*

CANADA

Eskimo

Saskatchewan

L. Winnipeg

ATLANTIC
OCEAN

Cascade Ra.

Columbia

Rocky Mts.

Snake

L. Superior

Missouri

L. Michigan

Ottawa

St. Lawrence

L. Huron

L. Ontario
Niagara Falls

L. Erie

Fur trapper

PACIFIC
OCEAN

Great Salt L.

UNITED STATES
OF AMERICA

Ohio

Appalachian Mts.

**Washington
DC**

*Grand
Canyon*

Arkansas

Mississippi

**American
Indian**

Rio Grande

MEXICO

Sierra Madre

*Gulf of
Mexico*

THE BAHAMAS

Cowboy

CUBA

*West
Indies*

Mexico City

*Caribbean
Sea*

Canada was settled by French and British
people in the 17th century and the country is
still divided into French and English speaking
regions.

The 19th and 20th century saw the arrival
of millions of immigrants from the United
Kingdom, Ireland, Italy, Greece, Poland and
many other countries, who came to North
America in search of a better life. Large
farms, many valuable mineral deposits, big
forests, rich fishing off the coasts and a wide
variety of fuels to power factories, have made
Canada and the U.S.A. very wealthy countries
where a lot of people enjoy a very high
standard of living.

*Panama
Canal*

*South
America*

| 0 | 1000 kilometres |
| 0 | 600 miles |

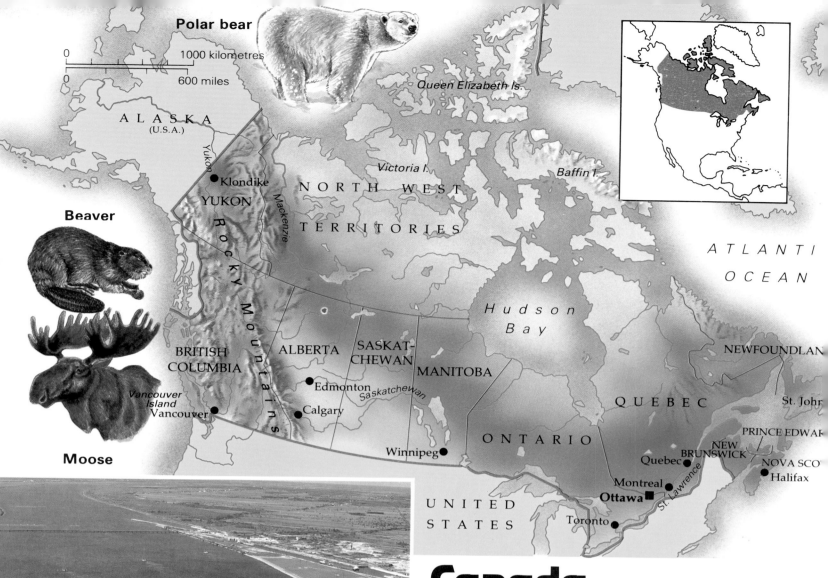

Polar bear

0 — 1000 kilometres
0 — 600 miles

Queen Elizabeth Is.

ALASKA (U.S.A.)

NORTH WEST

TERRITORIES

Victoria I.

Baffin I.

Klondike

YUKON

Beaver

ATLANTIC OCEAN

Hudson Bay

BRITISH COLUMBIA

ALBERTA

SASKAT-CHEWAN

MANITOBA

NEWFOUNDLAN

Edmonton

Saskatchewan

QUEBEC

St. Joh

Moose

Vancouver Island

Calgary

Vancouver

PRINCE EDWAR

NEW BRUNSWICK

Winnipeg

ONTARIO

Quebec

NOVA SCO

Halifax

Montreal

UNITED STATES

Ottawa

St. Lawrence

Toronto

Above: *The St. Lawrence has been dredged and deepened to allow ocean-going ships to sail into the lakes.*

Below: *The huge forests in British Columbia, Quebec and Ontario provide timber for the Canadian paper mills.*

Canada

Canada is a huge country, but vast areas in the cold, icy wastes of the north are completely uninhabited. Most of the people live in the south, near the border with the U.S.A.

In the southern half of Canada are the 'prairie provinces' of Manitoba, Saskatchewan and Alberta. The prairies are wide, flat plains where herds of buffalo used to roam. Now the prairies are covered in enormous fields of wheat, with cattle ranches in the drier areas.

Canada has many industries. They are mostly centred in the towns and cities around the Great Lakes and St. Lawrence river. Many of Canada's products are exported over the border to the U.S.A. or shipped abroad via the St. Lawrence seaway.

As well as processing food from the farms, fish from the rich fishing grounds off the Pacific and Atlantic coasts and timber from the forests, Canadian industries can use the many valuable minerals found in the country. These include iron ore, copper, gold, nickel, platinum and pitchblende (from which radium and uranium are extracted).

U.S.A.

Like Canada, the U.S.A. has rich farmlands and large deposits of minerals and fuels to feed her industries. The range of industries in the U.S.A. is enormous with every kind of product being manufactured.

The north-eastern corner of the U.S.A. is a very important industrial region. New York, Pittsburgh, Philadelphia, Baltimore, and the cities around the Great Lakes such as Buffalo, Detroit and Chicago, are all major manufacturing centres. A great network of roads, railways, canals and navigable rivers brings raw materials from the surrounding region. These materials include coal, iron ore, natural gas, oil and timber. The huge mechanized farms stretching west from Ohio to Kansas provide soya beans, wheat, maize, oats, hay and live-stock.

There is another important industrial region, right across on the western side of the U.S.A., around Los Angeles and San Francisco. The states on the west coast — Washington, Oregon and California — have valuable farmland too. California in particular produces large quantities of fruit and vegetables.

In the mountains of western U.S.A. mining

Above: *Tomato harvest in Florida. The warm climate brings tourists and means citrus fruits, sugar-cane and maize can be grown.*

is the chief occupation. Gold, silver, copper, lead, zinc and oil are all found in the Rockies. There are also huge sheep and cattle ranches.

Southern U.S.A. has an ideal climate for growing cotton, tobacco and maize. There are more and more industries growing up in the south. Large deposits of oil and natural gas around the Gulf of Mexico have made Houston, Galveston and Dallas into industrial centres.

Right: *Washington D.C. is the capital of the U.S.A. This is the White House where the President lives.*

Left: *The skyscrapers of New York City.*

Central America and the West Indies

Central America is a very mountainous region and the lower land around the coasts is hot and humid. Insects thrive in these conditions so the lowlands are often unhealthy and some of the main towns are up in the mountains where it is cooler.

Coffee is a very important crop in the highlands and bananas are grown in the lowlands. Both of these are cash crops, which means they are grown to be sold for money rather than to feed the local people. Most people live on the land, growing maize as their main food crop.

Mexico is by far the biggest country in this region. In the 1970s new deposits of oil were discovered in Mexico and this is helping Mexico to find the money to expand her industries and irrigate the drier areas. Tourists, from the U.S.A. in particular, also bring money into the country.

Right: *The Bahamas are a group of about 700 tiny islands. The tourist trade is very important. This picture shows how beautiful the beaches are.*

Left: *The Panama Canal joins the Atlantic and Pacific Oceans. The small state of Panama earns a lot of money from the canal.*

UNITED STATES

Tijuana

Sierra Madre

Gulf of California

Baja (lower) California

Monterrey

Gulf of Mexico

Tampico

MEXICO

Guadalajara

Mexico City

Acapulco

Yucatan Peninsula

BELIZE
Belmopan

GUATEMALA
Guatemala City
San Salvador
EL SALVADOR
HONDURAS
Tegucigalpa

NICARAGUA
Managua

San José
COSTA RICA

Panama Canal
Panama
PANAMA

PACIFIC OCEAN

Nassau
THE BAHAMAS

Havana
CUBA

DOMINI
RE

Port-au-Prince
Sa
Don

HAITI

G r e a t e r

JAMAICA Kingston

A

C a r i b b e a

COLOM

0   1000 kilometres

0   600 miles

Tourism is an important money-earner on many of the hot, sunny islands of the West Indies. There are also some large cash crops grown to be sold abroad, including coffee, sugar, cocoa and bananas. Cuba is one of the world's biggest sugar producers and also grows tobacco. This island has valuable deposits of nickel and iron ore too. Sugar is important in the Dominican Republic while coffee is the main export from Haiti. Both Haiti and Jamaica have reserves of bauxite — the ore from which aluminium is made.

Jamaica grows sugar, coffee and bananas

in the rich farmland around the edges of the island; the interior is very mountainous. The island is densely populated and many people have had to emigrate to seek work.

Barbados is also densely populated and sugar and sugar products make up the bulk of the island's exports. Trinidad grows sugar and cocoa but the island's oil deposits provide the main export. Puerto Rico has received a lot of aid from the U.S.A. and many Puerto Ricans have gone to live in America.

Some of the smaller islands of the West Indies produce limes and all of the islands grow maize and other foodstuffs. Many people still live off the land.

Above: *Sugar-cane is grown throughout the West Indies. The stems are cut and then processed in factories to produce sugar. Canes are stacked in bundles here.*

Right: *A market in Mexico.*

Below: *The West Indies got their name because when Christopher Columbus reached the islands in 1492 he thought he had sailed right around the world to India.*

Below: *A banana plantation in Honduras. Bananas and coffee are the chief export products of Honduras.*

South America

There are 13 countries in South America of which only one, French Guiana, is not now independent. It is a French colony. Suriname used to be ruled by the Netherlands and was called Dutch Guiana and Guyana used to be ruled by Britain and was called British Guiana. In the 16th and 17th centuries Brazil was colonized by Portugal and the other nine countries were colonized by Spain, but all these countries are now independent republics.

The very first people to live in South America probably came from Siberia, moving first into North America and then gradually spreading further south. When the first Europeans started exploring the continent in the 16th century they found these people living all over the continent. Among the most famous of these groups of Indians were the Incas who lived in the Andes in Peru.

Tapir

Howler monkey

Armadillo

Sloth

Caracas

Trinidad

V E N E Z U E L A

Orinoco

Georgetown

Paramaribo

GUYANA

Cayenne

Bogotá

SURI-NAME

FRENCH GUIANA

C O L O M B I A

Guiana Highlands

Negro

Quito

ECUADOR

Amazon

Amazon

Madeira

Tapajos

Xingu

B R A Z I L

Tocantins

Sao Francisco

P E R U

Lima

Cuzco

Brasilia

Brazilian Highlands

La Paz

B O L I V I A

Atacama Desert

Paraguay

PARAGUAY

Asunción

Salado

Parana

A T L A N T I C

O C E A N

Andes

Santiago

C H I L E

A R G E N T I N A

URUGUAY

Buenos Aires

Montevideo

Colorado

Patagonia

0   1000 kilometres

0   600 miles

Falkland Is.

Tierra del Fuego

Cape Horn

The Incas
The Incas lived in the Andes in Peru around their capital city of Cuzco. They constructed many beautiful buildings and made terraces for growing maize, potatoes and other crops. When the Spanish, under Francisco Pizarro, arrived in 1532 they killed the Inca ruler and destroyed this civilis-ation. Pizarro did not like living in Cuzco, so he moved down to the coast and founded the city of Lima.

As the first Europeans in South America were all men, they married Indian women, and their children, part European, part Indian, were known as Mestizos. Today, more South Americans are Mestizos than are pure blooded Indians or Europeans. The European settlers also brought Negroes from Africa and East Indians from Asia to work as slaves.

The Andes mountains run right down the western side of South America. The mountains in eastern South America — the Guiana and Brazilian Highlands — are much older and not as high as the Andes.

In between these areas of high ground are the big river basins. The river Orinoco in the north has formed a lowland area in Venezuela. The river Amazon and its tributaries run through the great Amazon basin. This low-lying, forested area covers more than three million square kilometres. In the south is the Plate estuary into which the Parana and Paraguay rivers flow. Their basins form a great plain sloping from the Andes to the coast.

South America has considerable mineral wealth, especially in the Andes and Guiana and Brazilian Highlands. The continent is changing from being a mainly agricultural land to being more highly industrialized.

Macaw **Giant anteater**

Right: *Brasilia is the capital of Brazil. The city was built in the 1950s to encourage people to move into the interior. The modern buildings are laid out in the shape of an aeroplane.*
Left: *The River Amazon flows through a huge area covered in thick jungle.*
Right: *Copper mining in Chile. Copper accounts for 80% of all Chile's exports.*
Below right: *People of the Andes. These Indians live in Peru.*

Countries of the Andes

The Andes are the longest range of mountains in the world, running right from the north to the south of the western side of South America. Travelling is very difficult in these mountainous regions as road and railways are very expensive and hard to build.

Venezuela was named after Venice in Italy as some early explorers found a marshy coastline similar to the area around Venice. The marshy area is Lake Maracaibo which is a major oil-producing region. This oil has made Venezuela one of the richest countries in South America and has provided the money for many new factories, roads and houses.

In both Venezuela and Colombia, cotton, coffee and cocoa are grown and cattle are raised. But farming is more important in Colombia as the country lacks Venezuela's valuable oil reserves. Coffee, in particular, is a very large crop in Colombia and a great deal is exported. There is also a textile industry, processing locally grown cotton.

In Ecuador, Bolivia and Peru there are high plateaux between the mountains where a large part of the population live. Most of the farmers are poor and can only grow enough to feed themselves. Their crops depend on the height of the mountain slopes.

On the coast of Ecuador, bananas, coffee and rice grow in the warm, moist climate. The coast of Peru, however, is a desert region where crops can only be grown at oases or with the help of irrigation. Fishing is very important off the coast.

Bolivia has no coastline but, like most of the other countries of the Andes, does have considerable mineral wealth in the mountains. Bolivia's biggest export is tin, but there are also deposits of copper, lead, zinc and gold.

Chile changes from very dry desert in the north to very wet, forested land in the south. Most people live in the middle of the country where there is enough rain to grow crops including wheat and fruit. Even so, Chile has

Inset opposite: *Lake Titicaca is high in the mountains on the border of Peru and Bolivia. The local people make boats of reeds.*

Below: *Llamas can live high up in the Andes and can be used to carry small loads.*

Crops grown in Andes

Above 2000 metres
Grassland, cold
Crop: wheat
Livestock: sheep, llamas

1000 to 2000 metres
Fewer trees, cooler
Crops: coffee, maize

Sea-level to 1000 metres
Forest, warm
Crops: cocoa, bananas, sugar-cane

Above: *Angel Falls in Venezuela is the highest waterfall in the world.*

to import a lot of food. The country is, however, rich in natural resources, particularly coal and copper. There is some oil and iron ore too. Most of Chile's population are now living in the towns where the growing number of factories attract people away from the land. The factories process the country's raw materials including grapes, wool, hides, wood and cotton as well as the many minerals.

L. Maracaibo

Caracas

VENEZUELA

Magdalena

Orinoco

Angel Falls

Bogotà

COLOMBIA

Quito

ECUADOR

Andes

BRAZIL

PERU

Lima

Cuzco

L. Titicaca

La Paz

BOLIVIA

Santa Cruz

Sucre

Atacama Desert

Andes

ARGENTINA

Valparaiso

Santiago

CHILE

Punta Arenas

Tierra del Fuego

Cape Horn

0   1000 kilometres

0   600 miles

Eastern South America

The huge country of Brazil covers nearly half of South America and the tropical forest of the Amazon Basin covers nearly half of Brazil. Most of the rest of the country is high, but flat, and cooler. More than half the population of South America live in Brazil, mostly on or near the coast.

VENEZUELA

Georgetown
GUYANA   Paramaribo
          SURINAME
              Cayenne
              FRENCH
              GUIANA

Guiana Highlands

Negro

Amazon   Manaus   Amazon   Belem

Madeira   Tapajos

Xingu

Tocantins   Recife

Sao Francisco

B R A Z I L   Salvador

Brasilia

BOLIVIA   B r a z i l i a n

H i g h l a n d s   A T L A N T I C

Paraguay   O C E A N

Parana

PARAGUAY   Sao Paulo
Asunción   Rio de Janeiro

CHILE

Salado

Parana   Uruguay

San Juan

Santa Fe   URUGUAY

Buenos   Montevideo
Aires

ARGENTINA   Mar del Plata
Colorado   Bahia Blanca

Negro

Patagonia

0   1000 kilometres

0   600 miles

Very few people live in the Amazon Basin. The difficulties of travelling through the forest and the hot, wet climate has discouraged settlers. The scattered groups of Indians who do live there lead very simple lives — hunting and fishing and sometimes clearing small areas for crops. More and more trees are now being cut down to build roads and to clear land for farming. Unfortunately the forest soil is poor and the farming is not always successful.

In the north-east of Brazil, around the coastal towns of Recife and Salvador, sugar-cane, bananas, tobacco and cocoa are grown. Further south, around Rio de Janeiro and São Paulo, coffee, cotton, oranges and sugar are all very important. Rio de Janeiro has a beautiful natural harbour and is the commercial centre of Brazil. São Paulo is the largest manufacturing city. Inland is a vast, sparsely populated area where cattle are grazed. There are some very large deposits of iron ore in this area as well as other useful minerals and gold and diamonds.

North of Brazil are the three small countries of Guyana, Suriname and French Guiana. All three are covered in dense forest and timber is a major export.

To the south of Brazil are the rich farm lands of Argentina, Uruguay and Paraguay.

Argentina is the second biggest country in South America and is very wealthy. The huge grasslands of central and northern Argentina are called the pampas. Here, deep, fertile soil means millions of cattle and sheep can be grazed, and wheat, maize and flax grown. Enormous quantities of meat, wool, hides and grain are exported and there are many big factories processing all the raw materials produced.

Uruguay is another rich agricultural nation. Four-fifths of the country is used as grazing for sheep and cattle and crops like rice, sugar beet and grapes are grown on the rest.

Paraguay also has rich soil and a good climate, but the country is not yet highly developed. There is no coastline which makes trading more difficult. The most important crop grown for sale abroad is cotton.

Right and below right:
South of the pampas is the very dry region called Patagonia. Very few people live here although there are some very large sheep farms.

Below: *An Indian from a tribe which live in the Mato Grosso — the second largest state in Brazil which borders Bolivia and Paraguay*

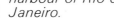

Left: *The beautiful harbour of Rio de Janeiro.*

Australasia

Australasia includes Australia, New Zealand and the neighbouring islands of the South Pacific Ocean.

The original inhabitants of Australia and New Zealand are thought to have travelled by boat from Asia thousands of years ago. The descendants of these people, the Aborigines and the Maoris, still live in Australia and New Zealand but they are now far outnumbered by settlers from Europe.

Dutch sailors first discovered Australia at the beginning of the 17th century. Abel Janszoon Tasman, a Dutch navigator, sailed around the southern coast in 1642. The island of Tasmania and the Tasman Sea are named after him.

In 1768 Captain James Cook sailed from England and eventually landed at Botany Bay near Sydney. A settlement followed here in 1788. Because it was such an isolated, desolate area, Britain established a penal settlement there, where convicts were sent to serve their sentences in very harsh conditions. Free settlers began arriving soon after, although the first European settlement in New Zealand did not take place until 1840.

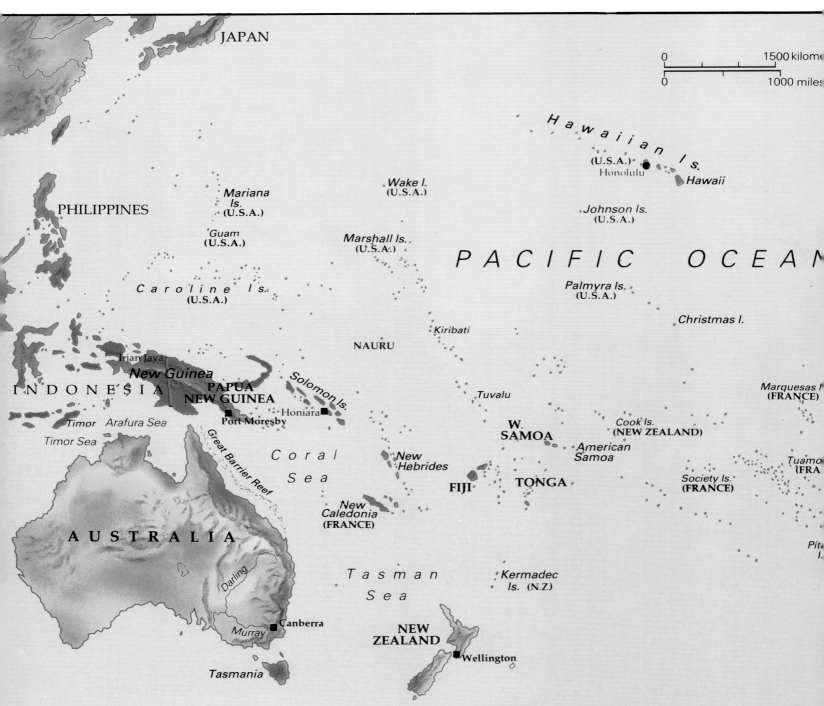

Before reaching Australia, Cook sailed around New Zealand. But when he tried to land on North Island the Maoris attacked his men and they were forced to retaliate.

Above: *Australian Aborigines originally lived by hunting and gathering roots and plants, moving about to find food. Nowadays few live like this and many have adopted the way of life of the Europeans who have emigrated to Australia. In the 1870s there were about 300 000 Aborigines in Australia. Now there is only one third of that number.*

NORTH AMERICA

Galapagos Is.
(ECUADOR)

SOUTH
AMERICA

Easter I.
(CHILE)

Australia

Australia is very large, nearly as big as Europe, but it has a much, much smaller population. Most of the people live in the large towns around the coast as the interior or 'outback' is very dry and dusty.

Where there is water in the outback there are enormous sheep and cattle stations often covering several thousand square kilometres. There are over 130 million sheep and about 30 million cattle in Australia. Huge quantities of wool and meat are produced.

Nearer the coast, crops, including wheat, sugar beet, oats and fruit can be grown. Irrigation schemes have helped to increase the amount of productive land.

Australia is very rich in natural resources being one of the world's leading mineral producers. As well as mining a wide variety of materials, of which the most important is iron ore, Australian governments have made great efforts to set up industries which will turn these raw materials into finished goods. Ships, cars and chemicals are all now manufactured.

Top: *A cattle station in Queensland.*
Above: *A sheep auction in New South Wales.*

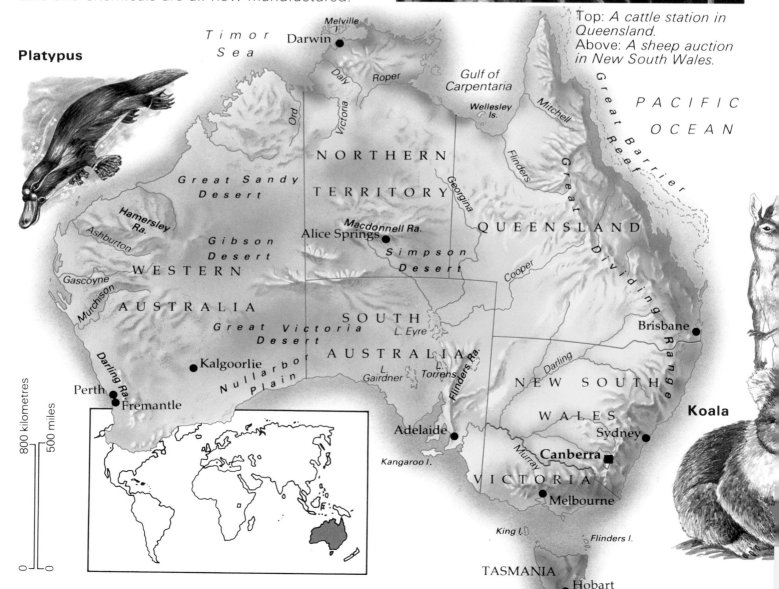

Platypus

Koala

Kangaroo

Emu

Wombat

Above: *An aerial view of a cattle station and homestead in Northern Territory. There is a billabong alongside the station.*

Inset: *Parliament House, Canberra. Canberra is the capital of Australia.*

Right: *Coober Pedy is a small town in South Australia where opals are mined. It is so hot that people have built their homes under the ground.*

63

New Zealand

New Zealand is made up of two main islands which together are about as big as the British Isles but they only have just over three million inhabitants.

Much of North Island is used for rearing dairy cattle and sheep and the farms are very efficient and successful. Cheese and butter are exported as well as meat.

South Island has a big range of mountains running down the west side. These are the Southern Alps which reach 3 764 metres at their highest point (Mount Cook) and contain many glaciers. There are several large fjords on the south-west coast.

The eastern side of South Island has a big expanse of rolling grassland known as the Canterbury Plains. This is an important sheep rearing and wheat producing area.

Like Australia, New Zealand is a wealthy country and has small deposits of gold and coal, as well as oil reserves. Hydro-electric and geothermal (using heat from beneath the earth's crust) power are also used.

Above: *Sheep grazing on the Canterbury Plains, beneath the Southern Alps.*

Above left: *Hot springs at Rotorua on North Island. The water is heated deep inside the earth and shoots up in the air as a geyser.*

Above: *Lake Tekapo in the Southern Alps.*

Left: *Christchurch cathedral. Christchurch is the biggest city on South Island and is a port and market centre for the Canterbury Plains.*

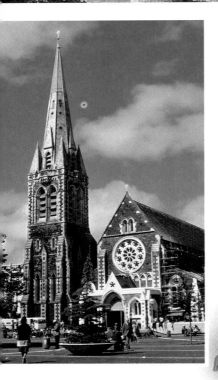

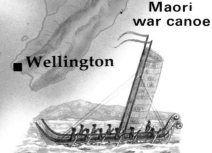

Kiwi

Auckland

Hamilton

Lake Taupo

Rotorua

North Island

Maori war canoe

Tasman Sea

Nelson

■ Wellington

Mount Cook ▲

Christchurch

Southern Alps

South Island

Invercargill

Dunedin

Stewart Island

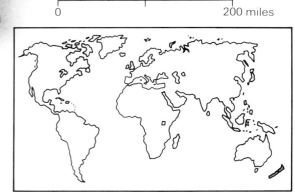

| 0 | | | 300 kilometres |
| 0 | | | 200 miles |

The Pacific Islands

An outrigger

There are thousands of islands in the Pacific Ocean. Some are volcanic, others are coral islands built up by the tiny coral animals.

The islands can be divided into three main groups — Melanesia, Micronesia and Polynesia — according to the kind of people who first lived there.

Melanesia means 'black islands'. This name arose because of the dark coloured skin of most Melanesians. These islands lie to the north and north-east of Australia and include the eastern part of New Guinea called Papua New Guinea. This region is covered in dense rain forests and has many high mountains so communications are very difficult.

Micronesia means 'small islands' and these are scattered all over the central Pacific Ocean. The inhabitants live mostly by fishing.

Easter Island, off the west coast of Chile, is famous for its huge stone statues.

Inset: *New Guinea tribesmen*

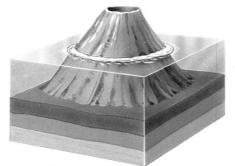

Polynesia means 'many islands'. These islands lie in a triangle between New Zealand, Hawaii and Easter Island. The Maoris of New Zealand are Polynesians. Fishing and tourism are important on the islands.

The Formation of a Coral Atoll

First coral grows around a volcanic island which has been thrown up from beneath the Earth's crust.

While the volcanic island sinks down the coral continues to grow up towards the surface.

If the volcanic island sinks completely, the coral is left as a ringlike coral island enclosing a lagoon — an atoll.

The Arctic

The Arctic is a region of sea almost completely surrounded by land. It is so cold that the sea around the North Pole is permanently frozen.

The land in the Arctic circle is called tundra. It is covered in snow and ice during the winter but in the short summer the snow on the surface melts and patches of moss and lichen grow and even, in some spots, carpets of beautiful flowers. But there are no trees and only a few stunted bushes. Even in the summer the temperature does not rise above 10°C.

The only people who live permanently in the Arctic are the Eskimos who used to live by hunting, fishing and trapping. Now western technology has reached them their old way of life is changing. The Lapps, who live in the northern forests of Scandinavia, herd their reindeer into the Arctic regions in the summer.

The discovery of oil and gas deposits and of other useful minerals may bring wealth to this previously undeveloped area.

Above: *Reindeer gathering in Lapland. Lapland is the northern most part of Norway, Sweden and Finland.*

66

Antarctica

Antarctica is a huge continent entirely covered by ice up to three kilometres thick. If this ice melted the sea level all over the world would rise by about 70 metres, submerging much of London, New York, Sydney and other cities.

The average annual temperature at the South Pole is about —49°C., and the average July (mid-winter) temperature is —75°C. Fierce winds blow and it is as dry as the Sahara desert. There are four to five months of continuous daylight in summer (November to February) and four to five months of continuous darkness in winter.

Not surprisingly the Antarctic has no permanent inhabitants but a number of manned scientific research camps and weather stations have been set up. Icebreakers are needed to supply these camps as the boats have to penetrate miles of ice to reach the land.

Huge reserves of oil and valuable minerals are thought to lie beneath the ice of Antarctica but as yet no one has discovered a way of reaching this wealth.

Above: *Adelie penguins in the Antarctic.*

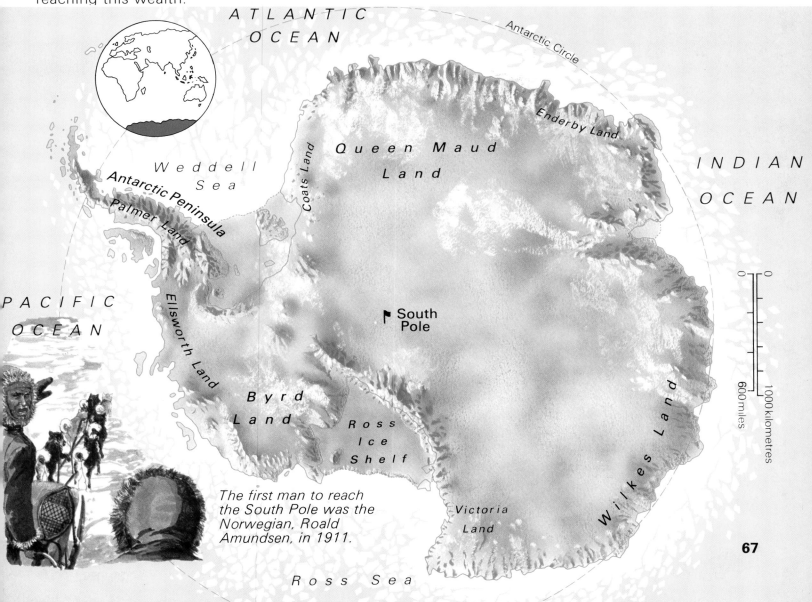

The first man to reach the South Pole was the Norwegian, Roald Amundsen, in 1911.

67

The Oceans

Water covers more than 70% of the Earth's surface and the average depth of the world's oceans is nearly 4 000 metres; some parts are over 11 000 metres deep. The oceans are shallowest around the edges of the land. These areas, where the water is less than 200 metres deep, are called the continental shelves. The deep ocean floors have a landscape as varied as the land above the water. There are mountains higher than Everest, great trenches much deeper than the Grand Canyon in the U.S.A., and vast plains of sand and mud.

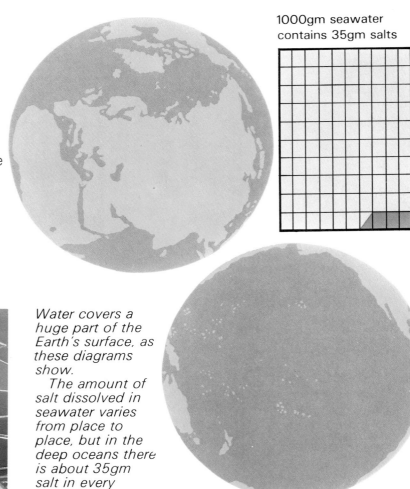

1000gm seawater contains 35gm salts

Above: *Saltpans in New Zealand. Seawater is trapped in shallow lakes and the heat of the sun evaporates the water leaving salt.*

Water covers a huge part of the Earth's surface, as these diagrams show.
The amount of salt dissolved in seawater varies from place to place, but in the deep oceans there is about 35gm salt in every 1000gm seawater.

The oceans and seas of the world have salty water. About 3.5% of the total volume of this water is actually made up of salts which are dissolved in the water. This average figure of 3.5% increases in very sunny conditions when water evaporates leaving the salts behind. Cold areas, where little evaporation takes place and where large rivers flow into the sea bringing fresh water, may be much less salty.

Currents and Tides

The oceans of the world are never still. Great 'rivers' of water move along the surface and beneath the oceans. These currents are driven by the wind and affected by the rotation of the Earth which turns the currents round to their right (in a clockwise direction) in the Northern Hemisphere, and to their left (anti-clockwise) in the Southern Hemisphere.

There are other movements of water called tides. These are caused by the gravitational attraction of the Moon and Sun. The Moon although much smaller than the Sun, has the greater influence because it is much nearer the Earth. Many parts of the world experience two high and two low tides every 24 hours.

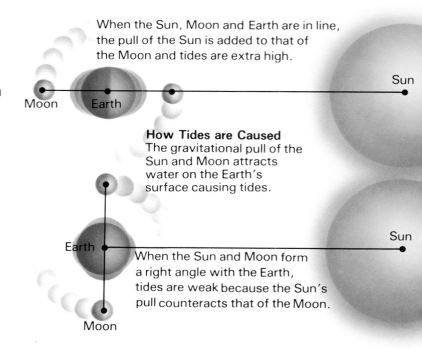

When the Sun, Moon and Earth are in line, the pull of the Sun is added to that of the Moon and tides are extra high.

Moon Earth Sun

How Tides are Caused
The gravitational pull of the Sun and Moon attracts water on the Earth's surface causing tides.

Earth Sun

When the Sun and Moon form a right angle with the Earth, tides are weak because the Sun's pull counteracts that of the Moon.

Moon

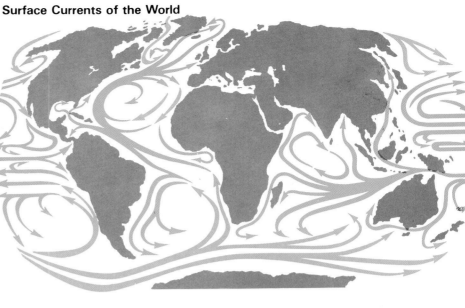

Above: *Currents have a big influence on climate. A warm current, like the one round the coast of Norway, can keep ports like Bergen ice-free.*

⟶ Warm surface currents

⟶ Cold surface currents

Wealth from the Oceans

The oceans of the world provide us with food, water and minerals. Some of the shallower seas are rich in plankton, which is the name given to the millions of tiny plants and animals floating around in the sea. Plankton is what a great many fish feed on, so where there is plankton there are also rich fishing grounds. The continental shelf areas around Iceland, the British Isles and Japan are some of the best fishing grounds in the world.

The oceans can also provide fresh water in areas where there is not much rain, if the sea-water is processed to remove the salt.

All the minerals found on and beneath dry land can also be found in the oceans of the world. Of course it is not always easy to extract these minerals, but as deposits on land are used up more countries are looking to find wealth beneath the oceans. Already large amounts of coal, oil and gas are extracted.

Fishing Grounds of the World

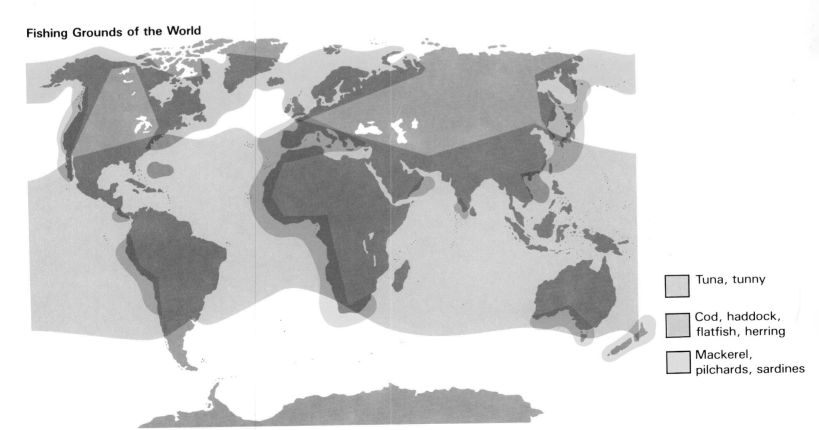

Tuna, tunny

Cod, haddock, flatfish, herring

Mackerel, pilchards, sardines

69

Index

Numbers in *italic* refer to names on maps.
Numbers in **bold** refer to illustrations.